# THE TWO SOVEREIGNTIES

# THE TWO SOVEREIGNTIES

## A STUDY OF THE RELATIONSHIP BETWEEN CHURCH AND STATE

*by*

JOSEPH LECLER, S.J.

PHILOSOPHICAL LIBRARY

NEW YORK

Published 1952
by the Philosophical Library, Inc.,
15 East 40th Street, New York 16, N.Y.

MADE AND PRINTED IN GREAT BRITAIN BY
WILLIAM CLOWES AND SONS LIMITED, LONDON AND BECCLES

# CONTENTS

Page

FOREWORD · vii

## Part One

# The Catholic Doctrine on Church and State

*Chapter*

I THE CHRISTIAN REVOLUTION IN REGARD TO SOVEREIGNTY — — — — — — — 3

II THE DISTINCTION BETWEEN CHURCH AND STATE 15

III AGREEMENT BETWEEN CHURCH AND STATE — 32

IV THE PRIMACY OF THE SPIRITUAL: ITS PRACTICAL EXPRESSION THROUGHOUT THE AGES — — 50

V THE PRIMACY OF THE SPIRITUAL: THEORIES OF INDIRECT POWER — — — — — 71

## Part Two

# Various Theories and Historical Situations
# Caesaro-Papism—Clericalism—The Lay State

VI CAESARO-PAPISM — — — — — 87

VII CLERICALISM — — — — — — 108

VIII THE LAY STATE — — — — — 128

   1. Can the secularization of the State be lawful? — — — — — — 129

   2. Modern Regalism — — — — 143

   3. Liberal Separatism — — — — 155

CONCLUSION — — — — — — — 182

v

# FOREWORD

CHURCH and State! In spite of the many books devoted to this complex subject, the problem is one which remains open to discussion; nor is it possible in a modest essay like the present to deal with all its aspects. It has consequently been thought best to treat only one of these aspects, but one of capital importance, namely the Church's attitude towards the question of State sovereignty.

To state that temporal sovereignty exists is to state the obvious. Differences of opinion may indeed arise about its origin or about the person or body incarnating it, but the fact that there is such a thing as State sovereignty can scarcely be called in question. Whether it is considered to reside in a nation, an individual or a group, it is a distinguishing mark of every State that is worthy of the name. It was doubtless not until modern times that the notion of sovereignty became the object of technical study and of controversy amongst lawyers, but it is already present in the Aristotelian and scholastic idea of the Perfect Society. It would also seem to be found in the old Roman notion of *imperium* which originally signified the supreme power of the King. It was used, in any given society, to mean the authority against which there is no appeal, or, to borrow M. Le Fur's phrase, that which has "the right of saying the last word".[1]

We shall try, then, to define the Church's position in relation to a temporal sovereignty, the rights and legitimate demands of which she desires to safeguard. We should feel that our object was gained if we succeeded in giving a clear picture of the finely balanced yet solid character of the Catholic thesis. It is thus only in its general principles that we propose to treat the problem of the relationship of things spiritual and temporal. This means that grave practical questions must be excluded from our discussion: the respective rights of Church and State over school and family, the relations of the Church with the

[1] L. Le Fur, *Les Grands Problèmes du Droit*, Paris, 1937, p. 294.

vii

international community, the temporal power of the Holy See, the relations of Catholic Action with political and professional activities, the personal attitude of the Christian towards temporal affairs. . . . It will be observed, none the less, that useful suggestions for the solution of such problems are to be found in these pages: whilst, if the reader requires supplementary information in regard to any of these delicate questions, he can obtain it from a number of excellent works already published.

There is no need for a long explanation of the plan followed in this work, a plan necessitated by the constructive object which we have had in view. The object of the first part is to explain the Catholic position, and we have not hesitated to describe as revolutionary the attitude taken up by the Primitive Church towards the Roman State. Nothing could have been more contrary to the ideas which were prevalent throughout the whole ancient world than the disassociation of the temporal from the spiritual, of the State from religion. Thus, starting from the "Christian Revolution," we establish the leading Catholic principle in regard to matters political, namely the complete autonomy, the distinct sovereignty, of the Church on the one hand and of the State on the other. Yet, real though this distinction between the two powers may be, it does not amount to radical separation, for it has to be reconciled with a second principle, that of the agreement and harmonization of the two for the common benefit of humanity. Finally the fact that Church and State are unequal by nature and in dignity introduces a third principle: that of the primacy of the spiritual power, the precise sense and scope of which have next to be examined. The main question to decide is whether the intrinsic superiority of the Church leaves the State with genuine power and jurisdiction.

A doctrinal synthesis on the above lines prepares the way for the second section of this work in the course of which certain episodes in history are studied in the light of Catholic principles. Although the chances of any reappearance of Cæsaro-papism seem slight, its evolution is here described at some length, for not only does it loom large in history, it has also several times given occasion to the Church to define her doctrine. The question of *Clericalism* is, on the other hand, of topical interest. This is not due to any particular clerical tendency on the part of the Church of to-day; but, in the face of the persistent accusations of her enemies, it has seemed worth while to examine the nature of this grievance, as it has appeared in history and as it appears at the present day. The gravest phenomenon in modern times is that of the *lay State*. To this matter we have given special attention. First we have had to ask ourselves whether there is any kind of secularization of the State which is compatible with Catholic principles, and to this question we have felt obliged to give an affirmative reply; the examination of certain concrete cases will permit us to decide in practice how far such secularization can safely be extended. The danger of secularism is that of refusing to acknowledge any limit to the State's powers. The lay State cares only for its temporal interests and judges all the acts of its rulers by this standard alone. If it is despotic and absolutist, it will ignore the Church in her capacity as a centre of spiritual life, whilst exercising over her visible organization a jealous and exclusive control: this is *modern Regalism*, a laicized form of Caesaro-papism. If the lay State is "liberal" in character, it will know nothing of the Church as such, but will simply place her on the same footing in common law as any private society: this is a solution which we describe as *Liberal Separatism*. Finally, in order that we may be able to appreciate, in the light of the reactions of the Holy See, the practical value and permissibility of separation, we have to distinguish it, when viewed as a juridical formula, from the separatist principles condemned by the Church.

We have given a large place to history in this doctrinal essay. Certain historians will reproach us for this, as though historical integrity were incompatible with the formulation of valid judgments on men and systems. Others will blame us for having tried to "draw lessons from history"; for it appears to them that no conclusions can be reached in this way. To us, on the other hand, it seems that the long experience of the Catholic Church constitutes a precious treasure, both for the Church's own children and for humanity in general. Her unity and cohesion, throughout so many centuries and in relation

with so many different régimes, give to this experience of hers a
unique and unchanging significance; and even though it be
true, as it doubtless is, that the events which have moulded
the Church's history throughout the ages do not always provide
the data essential for the positive solution of present-day
problems, at least they serve as a warning of the faults to be
avoided and of the errors into which we should be careful not
to fall.

Recourse to history reveals itself, in fact, to be an indispensable factor in any serious attempt to find a solution of the
problems raised by the relationship between the two powers.
It allows us, as we survey the Church's attitude along the
centuries, to distinguish between the elements that are constant
and those that are transient, between solidly-founded tradition
and merely provisional orientations. There are certain acts by
the spiritual power which the circumstances and peculiar
conditions of a given civilization may justify but which one
must be careful not to erect into a universal norm, as though
they expressed a permanent right. For instance, when once we
understand properly the position of the Church in the Middle
Ages, we shall easily avoid drawing from it exaggerated
conclusions in regard to the general powers of the Papacy.
We must remember that Catholic dogma and discipline involve
a constant and true progress; it is not an evolution exposed to
every sort of risk; it is, literally, a development. Thus it was
but gradually that the Church succeeded in hitting upon a
happy mean of action between two possible dangers: that of
losing all contact with the world, so remaining without effect
upon it, and that of entering too much into worldly affairs,
thus risking a fall from spirituality. History alone will enable
us to trace the course of the Church's successive experiments
and to appreciate their significance. It will help us to see clearly
the development of policy through the changing character of
events.

*Part One*

# The Catholic Doctrine
# on Church and State

# I

# THE CHRISTIAN REVOLUTION
# IN REGARD TO SOVEREIGNTY

In the language of every day, which takes but little account of juridical distinctions, Church and State are two autonomous authorities, two distinct and sovereign societies. After so many centuries of Christianity the acts and attitudes of these two powers are such as abundantly to justify, and more than to justify, this mode of expression. History is indeed full of the conflicts between the two, of their struggles for influence and domination. Their agreements, their "concordats," may perhaps, in so far as external appearances are concerned, call to mind important international treaties. Even their very "separations" remind us of the behaviour of two rivals who, having failed either to agree with or to conquer the other, decide to ignore each other completely. The sovereignty of the Church within her own sphere is so well recognized to-day that a whole bevy of ambassadors is accredited to the Holy See!

There was a time, however, when this lawful claim on the Church's part was widely regarded as a scandal, an unheard-of and threatening novelty. In order to convince ourselves of this, we need only look backward to the early days of the Church's life, to the times of Christ and of primitive Christianity. We shall then see at work a spiritual revolution which cut at the very roots of the ancient notion of the State.

There is one famous saying of Our Lord's which writers on the Church's relations with the temporal power always delight in quoting. The circumstances are familiar to all. Some Pharisees and Herodians approached the Master one day with a view to catching Him out in His speech. "Is it right," they

3

asked Him, "to pay tribute to Caesar or not?" This was an insidious and a treacherous question; for if He replied yes, He would lose the good opinion of the Jews who were dreaming of a national liberator, whilst if He replied no, He would appear in the eyes of the Roman authorities as a fanatic and a rebel. Knowing their malice, Jesus simply said: "Bring me a *denarius*." This was the tribute-money and, when it had been brought, He glanced at it and asked a question in His turn: "Whose is this likeness? Whose name is inscribed on it?" "Caesar's," they said. Whereupon He answered: "Why, then, give back to Caesar what is Caesar's and to God what is God's." In other words: "You use this money, that is to say, in practice you recognize the Emperor; give him then what belongs to him but without forgetting what you owe to God."[1]

This reply has not, by itself, the full significance ordinarily attributed to it, for it could be taken to refer solely to the rights of the religious conscience and its inescapable duties. Nor was it the first time in history that the attention of the civil powers had been drawn by an elect soul to the requirements of the Law of God. For, not to mention Plato, and Sophocles' *Antigone*, had not Cicero himself pointed out that there is in our consciences an unwritten, unchanging, eternal law "from which we cannot be set free either by the Senate or by the people"?[2] It is only indeed in the light of one all-important fact that it is possible for us to appreciate the decisive significance of these words; and this fact is that Christ is not merely the initiator of a powerful spiritual movement, He is the Divine Founder of an organized, hierarchical visible Church, totally distinct, both in its methods and in its final end, from an ordinary political society.

The proclamation of the Kingdom of God takes a central place in the Gospel message. Now, what is this Kingdom which is mentioned so often in the Master's parables and teachings? The Sermon on the Mount presents it to us as a great religious entity unconnected with temporal goods. Its subjects do not amass for themselves treasures which can be corrupted by moth or rust, or stolen by thieves. Riches are an obstacle rather than an aid to entering that Kingdom. Poverty, renunciation, detachment from all earthly things are the surest means of attaining to it. True, it can be taken by storm—*regnum Dei vim patitur*—but the violence here referred to is of the soul, it has to do with Christian ascetics and the arduous paths of penance. And this Kingdom has no more relationship with temporal domination than it has with the riches that perish. To the Tempter who offers Our Lord all the kingdoms of the world with all their glory, provided that He will adore him, Christ replies with words of scornful indignation. He has not come to proclaim a political Kingdom but a Kingdom that is to be both spiritual and universal: "This Gospel of the Kingdom shall be preached in the whole world to be a witness to all nations." Of this Kingdom He has no hesitation in proclaiming Himself to be the Chief and King. He does not contradict Nathaniel's spontaneous exclamation: "Thou art the King of Israel!" whilst to Pilate's question He replies unhesitatingly: "I am a King," though adding: "My Kingdom is not of this world." His acts, moreover, bear witness to this fact. He scorns all riches, so far as He Himself is concerned, and has no stone whereon to lay His head. To the disciples, anticipating His glorious exaltation, He announces His sufferings and death, and, faced by enthusiastic throngs who propose to make Him King, He hides Himself and takes refuge in flight.

Nevertheless, however spiritual it may appear to be, the Kingdom of Christ does assume a social and organic form. The parables compare it to a vineyard into which the father of the family sends vinedressers; they liken it also to an agricultural settlement administered by a steward and to a flock guarded by a shepherd. Nor is it a purely heavenly society which is here described to us, some future community of the eschatological order: it is to grow upon this earth and to develop, like a mustard seed which becomes a tree, and, just as cockle and wheat are found side by side in the same field, it includes both righteous and unrighteous members. An hierarchical organization is to preside over its growth and its destinies in this world. The misdeeds of the faithful are to be rendered liable to punishment. In fact, it is with this end in view that the Apostles are invested with effective authority: they are to pronounce sentences which will be confirmed by

God Himself. "Whatsoever you shall bind on earth shall be bound in Heaven, and whatsoever you shall loose on earth shall be loosed in Heaven." Above the Apostles again, Peter is appointed visible Head of the Kingdom which Christ on this occasion calls His "Church". He is the foundation whence the whole edifice obtains its coherence and its stability: he is the prime minister who bears the "Keys of the Kingdom of Heaven"; he is the supreme judge to whom all have the right of final appeal.

It is in the light of these new ideas that the words of Christ about obedience to Caesar should be interpreted. We are thus made to realize that the Apostles do not merely acquire a strong personal conviction of their duties towards God; they also find themselves committed, quite consciously, to accepting two sets of social obligations. On the one hand, as citizens—members of a human and terrestrial city—they owe submission to Caesar, and their loyalty is all the more sincere because they see in God the origin of secular authority in accordance with the words of Christ to Pilate: "Thou wouldst not have any power over Me at all, if it had not been given thee from above."[3] On the other hand, as Christians they expect to achieve the salvation of their souls through adhesion to a spiritual, but none the less visible, society which Christ has provided with a doctrine, an hierarchical organization and the means of sanctification. In case of any conflict, a general rule is laid down for them: "God is greater than Caesar!" and the authority of the spiritual shepherds will suffice to recall to the faithful the duty of resistance—we will not say revolt—when the exigencies of Caesar are in disaccord with the Law of God.

The Apostles shaped on the same lines the religious society founded by Christ. Like their Master, they had every intention of rendering to Caesar what was Caesar's due. St. Peter and St. Paul in their letters inculcated upon the faithful the duty of respectful submission to the established powers:

Every soul [wrote St. Paul] must be submissive to its lawful superiors; authority comes from God only, and all authorities that hold sway are of His ordinance. Thus, the man who opposes authority is a rebel against the ordinances of God, and rebels secure their own condemnation. A good conscience has no need to go in fear of the magistrate as a bad conscience does. If thou wouldst be free from the fear of authority, do right and thou shalt win its approval; the magistrate is God's Minister, working for thy good. Only if thou dost wrong, needest thou be afraid; it is not for nothing that he bears the sword; he is God's Minister still, to inflict punishment on the wrongdoer. Thou must needs then be submissive, not only for fear of punishment, but in conscience. It is for this same reason that you pay taxes; magistrates are in God's service and must give all their time to it. Pay every man then his due; taxes if it be taxes, customs if it be customs; respect and honour if it be respect and honour.[4]

For love of the Lord then [wrote St. Peter in his turn], bow to every kind of human authority; to the King who enjoys the chief power, and to the magistrates who hold his commission to punish criminals and encourage honest men. To silence by honest living the chatter of fools, that is what God expects of you. Free men, but the liberty you enjoy is not to be made a pretext for wrongdoing; it is to be used in God's service. To God, your reverence; and to the King, due honour.[5]

The firm tone of these instructions leaves us in no doubt regarding the loyalty of the two great Apostles towards the temporal city: but they were none the less engaged in building, with incredible energy, an autonomous spiritual city recognizing no distinction between class or nation:

No more Jew or Gentile; no more slave and freeman, no more male and female, you are all one person in Jesus Christ.[6]

This spiritual city is doubtless built primarily upon a principle of mystic unity: it is the "Body of Christ"; but it also possesses a visible unity of its own, it has its rulers and its government. St. Paul, like St. Peter, teaches, commands and reprimands. He claims the right to chase recalcitrant sinners from the Christian community, that is, the right of excommunication.[7] He even goes so far as to blame the faithful for submitting their disagreements to the pagan Courts of Law; the heads of the Christian communities, he tells them, are perfectly competent to settle such disputes.[8] And in fact the subordinate pastors do exercise their jurisdiction under the general authority of the Apostles. "Keep watch then over yourselves," said St. Paul to the "Ancients" of Miletus, "and over God's Church in which the Holy Spirit has made you bishops. You are to be shepherds of that flock which He won for Himself at the price of His own blood."[9]

No political aims, no dreams of temporal dominion, have a place in the minds of the organizers of the Church. The City which they found is not a "great power" in the earthly sense of the term; its citizens demand no rights save that of bearing witness to the Truth. In this sphere, however, the Church is sovereign. She denies the State all right to dictate to man the attitude which he is to adopt towards the mystery of the Unseen; it is her mission, and hers alone, to reveal to him the splendour of his destiny and the designs which God has formed for his spiritual life.

*　　　*　　　*

The introduction of a dualism of this kind between religious society and civil society represented in the ancient world a revolution without precedent. The incorporation of Religion in the State was in the cities of antiquity so incontestable a fact that it is useless to insist at any length upon it. Cicero put the whole matter in a nutshell when he wrote: "*Sua cuique civitati religio est, nostra nobis.*"[10] In the Roman Empire, in particular, no self-governing religious body was allowed to exist over against the State. The priests of the official religion were merely State functionaries entrusted with the performance of acts of worship; they were in no sense considered to be the custodians of doctrine; they were not even the people whom it was usual to consult in regard to religious questions. Moreover, the worship of the gods of Rome was a part of one's civic duty: it was required of all loyal subjects. Conquered peoples were indeed allowed to retain their national deities, and the diffusion throughout the Empire of certain cults of Oriental origin was permitted—but on one condition—those who embraced these foreign religions must retain their loyalty to the official gods. Thus while syncretism was allowed in religious matters, exclusiveness was forbidden. Men were allowed to worship

Mithra or Cybele, but only as long as they did not abandon the Roman deities; and when, in the second century, the cult of the Emperor in person had been definitely established, it was henceforth imposed upon all as a rigorous obligation.

In the ancient world even Judaism itself was not an exception. Its ethnical and national character always differentiated it from a purely spiritual society. Men speak of a "Jewish Church" because of the universalist tendencies apparent in the religion of Israel at the opening of the Christian era; but the expression is incorrect.

> In reality [writes Father Bonsirven[11]] these appearances of universalism are placed at the service of national particularism and serve to reinforce it. The observances of the cult, all of which were imposed upon the proselytes, were of a character no less ethnical than religious: their inevitable effect was to separate and, as it were, cut off the proselyte from his country of origin and his own race, in order to incorporate him in the Jewish nation.

We cannot but recall, whilst we are on this subject, the tragic misunderstanding which resulted in the opposition to Christ of the Pharisees of His time. Jesus proclaimed a Kingdom of God which would be a spiritual society; His hearers, for their part, persisted in linking together in their minds political dreams with Messianic hopes. After nineteen centuries of Christianity, we are inclined to blame very severely the lack of intelligence shown in this matter by the contemporaries of Christ. In fact, however, like all the men of antiquity, they were blinded by their ancestral traditions. Why, in order that the Apostles themselves might receive enlightenment, no less an event was required than the descent of God the Holy Ghost!

There is thus no exaggeration in speaking of a "Christian Revolution" where the matter of sovereignty is concerned. In the days before Christianity the world knew of one sovereignty only, that of the State, which exercised its sway alike on religious and on civil life, on the spiritual and on the temporal. With the advent of Christianity this unity was destroyed.

> The original contribution of Christianity [writes M. G. Renard] is the organization of the rights of conscience by

means of the establishment of an external society, perfect and endowed with a sovereignty like that of the State—the rival of the State. The Church, regarded from this point of view, is a juridical and political institution intended to protect the freedom of conscience even of those who have not the souls of heroes; the institution of the Church implies a fundamental separation of the spiritual and temporal domains: a division or "decentralization" of sovereignty. Since Christianity came, sovereignty has not only been "decentralized in respect of territories", it has also been "decentralized in respect of functions"; since Christianity came, the doctrine of relativity has affected sovereignty.[12]

As a result of the triumph of Christianity, that ancient absolutism which turned religion into a mere creature of the State was destined to undergo an assault of a decisive character; and this assault, pacific though it was—for the Church has never advocated sedition or armed revolt—provoked a formidable defensive reaction on the part of the State. The history of the Church up to the conversion of Constantine gives proof of this, and we can sum it up in one word; it is a history of *persecutions*. Nor is the fact that the Christians were thrown to the lions and hunted to death in a thousand different ways to be explained merely by the absurd fables which the pagans spread abroad at their expense. It is not to be explained merely by their monotheism or by their scorn of Caesar-worship, for the Jewish nation, which also rejected with horror this supreme form of idolatry, received tolerant treatment. The explanation lies rather in pagan recognition of the fact that, behind Christian universality, lay the complete and absolute negation of the State's claim to sovereignty in religious matters. As a matter of policy, the Emperors could allow a conquered nation, still shuddering from the blows it had received, to maintain with jealous care the exclusive cult of Yahweh. They felt bound however to proscribe a new sect which, after detaching itself from all national ties, had constituted itself into a spiritual city and was now calling into question an essential element of sovereignty. It was in vain that the defenders of the Christians praised their pacific spirit, their readiness to be taxed, their devotion to the Empire; their enemies merely replied by asking what was the use of all this parade of loyalty if the Christians claimed the right, in their capacity as a spiritual and universal society, to cut adrift from the State and the national deities? We do not of course deny for a moment either the injustice or the brutality of the persecutions, but it is easy to picture the alarm of the pagan magistrates when faced with a growing sect which proclaimed itself to be universal like the Empire and which, at the same time, threatened one of the pillars of the ancient State: its religious authority.

In any case these two centuries and a half of persecutions were not unprofitable to the Church, for during this time she was forced to rely only on herself, on the self-sacrifice of Christians and on their spirit of faith. The Church grew and developed in hostile surroundings with no support of any kind from outside. This could not but result in the strengthening of her internal cohesion and in a growing consciousness of her own autonomy. If the young Christian community had immediately become the ally of the State, she would have run a great risk of being absorbed sooner or later by her too intimate and too powerful partner. Her long trial was thus providential. When hostilities ceased and Caesar had himself embraced Christianity the essential independence of the spiritual power would be taken for granted. It would thenceforth be accepted by mankind as a solid and lasting acquisition.

*       *       *

This must not, however, be taken to mean that the revolution brought about by Christianity in the sphere of sovereignty, that the establishment of the dual control of Church and State, was to be proved by events to have furnished a solution free of all difficulty. So far is this from being true that religious history has for nineteen centuries been one long record of the incessant struggles between the spiritual and the temporal powers. Nothing could be more precarious, nothing more unstable, than the balance struck between them.

Scarcely had the ancient Christian epoch come to a close when the "peace of the Church" was interrupted by one

storm after another. These first clashes already foreshadowed
in their essential character the rivalries that were to come:
the expansion of one of the powers concerned beyond its due
limits; protests by the other power, and doctrinal conflicts;
active antagonisms, sometimes developing into real hostilities.
At that period, the still youthful Church was primarily concerned with the need of defending herself against her Imperial
protector. Things were different in the Middle Ages when the
spiritual power of the Church had increased as a result of her
obtaining an effective hold upon temporal affairs. From the
twelfth century onwards, in addition to the long rivalry
between the Papal and Imperial Courts, clashes began to
occur between the Church and the young national monarchies.
The tragic dispute between Thomas à Becket and Henry II
of England, the quarrel between Philip the Fair and Boniface
VIII, are still remembered. Modern political history, for its
part, has taken the form of a new thrust by the protagonists
of State-supremacy against the independence of the spiritual
power. The victory of the lay authorities was complete in the
countries which accepted the Reformation, England and the
German realms. Elsewhere, in the nations which remained
Catholic, the Church continued to exist as a distinct juridic
entity but she has never ceased, even up to our own day, to
experience the hostility, patent or latent, of the secular powers.
The tussles of Louis XIV with the Holy See, the anti-clerical
policy of the "enlightened" sovereigns, the French Revolution
and the Civil Constitution of the Clergy, the struggle between
Pius VII and Napoleon, finally in our own day the Law of
Separation: what are all these but the least unmistakable
symptoms of a profound and ineradicable antagonism?

Such, in brief, is the situation created in the world by this
double sovereignty. Nothing could be more deplorable, we
may feel like saying. It looks as though no lasting harmony
were possible between the Church and the temporal power.
Are we to conclude, then, that the Christian "revolution" has
failed where the question of sovereignty is concerned and that,
far from bringing peace to men, it has introduced instead into
political society, into civilization itself, a constant factor of
trouble and instability? So far back as the days of Rousseau

this highly plausible objection was put into words in the *Contrat Social* (iv.8):

> Jesus came to establish a spiritual kingdom on earth; and this, by separating the theological system from the political system made the State cease to be one, and gave rise to those internal divisions which have never ceased to rend the Christian peoples . . . The result of this dualism has been a perpetual conflict about jurisdiction which has rendered sound politics impossible in Christian States; whilst no one has ever been able to reach a conclusion as to which of the two we are obliged to obey, priest or temporal lord.

Auguste Comte, it is true, in his *Cours de Philosophie Positive*, takes the contrary view and maintains that the distinction of the spiritual from the temporal, in that it has introduced morals into politics, has done good service to the cause of social progress.[13] But all the defenders of the absolute sovereignty of the State are on the side of Rousseau and repeat the same argument: the co-existence in the same State of two independent jurisdictions can only give rise to disorder and confusion.

In order to reply to this objection, it now becomes necessary to set out in detail the Catholic teaching on the two sovereignties—by so doing we shall discover the fundamental reasons which in our eyes justify their radical duality.

### NOTES TO CHAPTER I

1 Matt. xxii. 16–22.
2 Cicero, *Republic*, Bk. III, quoted by Lactantius, *Institutiones Divinae*, VI, 8; edition Brandt, Vienna, 1890, p. 508.
3 John xix. 11.
4 Romans xiii. 1–7. It is quite evident that in this text St. Paul is not dealing with extraordinary cases, such as those which are produced by political revolutions. He is here simply envisaging the circumstances in which temporal authority is normally exercised.
5 I Peter ii. 13–17.
6 Galat. iii. 28.
7 II Cor. xiii. 1–2, 10. I Cor. v. 4–5. I Tim. i. 20.

[8] I Cor. vi. 1, 6.

[9] Acts xx. 28.

[10] Cicero, *pro Flacco*, 28.

[11] J. Bonsirven, *Le Judaisme palestinien au temps de Jésus-Christ*, Paris, 1935, I, p. 33.

[12] G. Renard, *L'Église et la Souveraineté*, in *La Vie Intellectuelle*, 1932, p. 14.

[13] A. Comte, *Cours de Philosophie Positive*, 5th edition, Paris, 1894, Vol. V, p. 263.

# II

# THE DISTINCTION BETWEEN
# CHURCH AND STATE

GENERALLY speaking, the Catholic doctrine of Church and State can be reduced to a few principles which, although apparently simple, require skill in interpretation. We find them expressed synthetically in a passage of Leo XIII's Encyclical on Christian marriage (*Arcanum*, 10 February, 1880):

> No one can doubt [wrote Pope Leo XIII] that the Divine Founder of the Church, Christ Jesus, desired ecclesiastical authority to be *distinct* from civil authority and that each should be free and in a position to carry out its own mission, with this proviso, however, which is useful to each of the two powers and which safeguards the interests of humanity, that agreement and harmony shall prevail between them, and that, in questions which fall beneath the judgment and jurisdiction of both—even though under different aspects— *the power which has charge of things human shall depend*, in a suitable and seemly manner, *on that which has received the guardianship of things divine.*

In this comprehensive sentence we find united the three principles by which the Catholic Church is guided in her relations with secular powers: a well-marked distinction between Church and State, the necessity of their being habitually in agreement, the dependence of the State in regard to the Church in mixed questions and in matters common to both. We shall examine these points in order.

A unique sovereignty, embracing Divine Worship and religious affairs in general, would probably be the normal thing in human society apart from any supernatural revelation.

In such a world-order, men, enlightened solely by reason, would organize, in accordance with their lights, Divine Worship and religious discipline. There would be nothing to stop them from entrusting to the lay authorities the custody of doctrine and the control of worship. The last end of man, St. Thomas points out, is to attain to the enjoyment of God: "If man were able to attain this end by means of his unaided nature, it would necessarily be part of the ruler's function himself to direct its subjects towards this end."[1] "In a humanity left to its own resources," writes in his turn the Jesuit Suarez,[2] "in a world without revelation, the religious power, like the political power, would spring from the sovereign community; and in order to exercise these two powers the latter would be free to set up either two administrations or a single one which, in these circumstances, would be clothed with a dual authority." The religious jurisdiction of the States of antiquity, continues the same theologian, is partly based on this hypothesis and in places which have not yet received the Gospel message external worship is left to man's initiative whilst its public manifestations are, as such, controlled by the body politic. Even in the Jewish world, the spiritual power was never independent in the full sense, it never constituted a Church. The ancient law, imperfect and transitory as it was, required no such dualism.

From the Christian point of view, then, dualism in sovereignty is not based solely upon the requirements of human nature. The origin and cause of the revolution brought about by Christ is to be found in the supernatural character of His Gospel, and in the irruption of the Divine into our world of sense. We may evoke in this connexion the vigorous antithesis of the Sermon on the Mount—"You know that it was said to men of old time . . . But I say to you. . . ." It was by means of startling rhythmic formulae of this kind that Jesus contrived to lay powerful stress on the amazing originality of His message. He was no longer teaching in the name of simple human reason or in that of common-sense principles of social justice. He was making known to the world the merciful designs of the Father and the mysteries of the Kingdom of Heaven; in return He was asking from man the free adhesion of an act of faith.

In the sphere of the natural order, as we have just seen, each State is able to fix, according to its own lights, the moral and religious attitude to be adopted by members of the city. It will take for its standard and its guide current ideas—always subject to revision and capable of improvement—on the dignity of man and on his duties towards God. In the new order established by Christ, things are otherwise. A truth which is absolute, albeit mysterious, has to be announced by Christ's representatives to humanity at large: "You must therefore go out, making disciples of all nations and baptizing them in the Name of the Father and of the Son and of the Holy Ghost, teaching them to observe all the commandments that I have given you."[3] This new and complete truth is not opposed to reason but it transcends reason whilst at the same time being such as to satisfy the most profound aspirations of man. In order that this truth may be held fast, that it may be preached to men, that it may be preserved in its authentic purity, a distinct authority, especially established by God, is required. Moreover, Christianity is not simply a body of supernatural doctrines and a community of believers; it is the Divine Life which has come into human souls to purify and sanctify them; and this Divine Life is given to them by means of a number of sensible signs and external rites.[3] As a super-natural *magisterium* is required in order to teach to the Faithful the mysteries of God, there is need of a priesthood deriving from no human source, to organize worship and to administer the Sacraments. We are thus enabled to see clearly, in the light of Revelation, the need for a spiritual society, radically distinct from the State, endowed with a triple authority—doctrinal, sacramental and legal—the object of which is to guide humanity to the vision of God, to a beatitude which could never be attained merely by means of the lights and energy proper to man's unaided Nature. Such a society as this does not act as a substitute for the temporal city, it establishes itself upon a higher plane. The State, under these new conditions of earthly existence, is not dispossessed of its essential prerogatives but it sees limits fixed to its power in the moral and religious sphere. It is no doubt true that, on any hypothesis, there are limits to political power. No man, even the

Head of a State, has a right to be unconditionally the master of another man. No earthly authority can disregard, without injustice, the inalienable rights of the human person. There has never been a time, even under the States of antiquity, when noble consciences have not protested against certain forms of tyranny. But since the coming of Christ, not only individual consciences but a spiritual society has had the task of placing, in God's Name, a limit to the rights of the secular power. The dualism of Church and State is undoubtedly a necessary consequence of the Christian Revelation and of the new conditions laid down for our salvation.

\*       \*       \*

This divided sovereignty has not simplified, it must be admitted, the tasks of government. Must we condemn it, then, on the grounds that, during nineteen centuries, perpetual tension has seemed to reign between Church and State? Is it true that this dualism of the spiritual and temporal powers, however legitimate in theory, leads in practice to nothing but sterile and disheartening conflicts? We do not think so. There is in fact, in this very tension, a precious safeguard for the personality of man and his higher interests.

In his work on "Traditional Social Science" Hauriou points out that a plurality of powers tends to safeguard personal liberty. "Every complete organization," he says, "is a sealed box, it is a prison for the individual. Society has discovered a very simple means of freeing itself by multiplying the number of organizations entitled to lay claim upon the same individual. The latter can play off one against the other, can obtain the protection of one against the other."[4] These ideas of Hauriou have made considerable progress since 1896, and the legal experts of our own day, reverting to the principle of Montesquieu that power alone can check power, tend to favour the limitation of the rights of the State by large autonomous communities with which the former would have to reckon.

Canon Law in the Middle Ages [writes M. Le Fur[5]] at least in so far as questions of the moral and religious order are concerned, had the effect of putting a check upon the juridical supremacy of the State, and we find to-day that a somewhat similar state of affairs prevails in regard to the modern State which calls itself "the lay State" and has given up all theocratic pretensions. International law has for some years now been engaged in fixing ever narrower limits to the sovereignty of the State, sometimes even in regard to questions of internal legislation (protection of minorities, international recognition of the Rights of Man) and soon perhaps a new organization, a new legal and social order, will be in a position to control economic life; we seem indeed to be tending more and more towards a plurality of sovereignties, each power having the right of final decision in its own sphere and being faced, in case of a conflict, with the necessity of reaching some agreement with equally independent neighbouring powers.

These views are interesting as marking a very definite reaction against State absolutism. They pave the way for a return of modern thought towards the traditional ideas of the Church about the necessity of maintaining a balance between the two great powers of this world. We may note in this connexion what Pope Gelasius wrote towards the end of the fifth century:[6]

Before the advent of Christ, of whom they were a figure, there were, as Holy Scripture tells us, men who were really priests and kings at the same time, such as Melchisedech . . . But since the true Priest-King has appeared, the emperor has no longer assumed the title of pontiff, nor has the priest claimed the royal dignity . . . Christ, in fact, out of consideration for human weakness, was careful to adopt, with wonderful wisdom, the measures most fitted to ensure the salvation of His own. *Wishing then to save those that believed in Him by the medicine of humility, instead of exposing them anew to the danger of perdition by the seductions of pride, He has divided the functions of the two powers, assigning to each one its proper task and dignity.* The spiritual power keeps itself detached from the snares of this world and, fighting for God, does not become entangled in secular affairs, while the secular power, for its part, refrains from exercising any authority over Divine affairs. *By thus remaining modestly within its own sphere, each power avoids the danger of pride which would be implicit in the possession of all authority and acquires a greater competence in the functions which are properly its own.*

Thus, in the eyes of Pope Gelasius, dual sovereignty is a permanent remedy against that radical vice of human nature: the tendency towards tyranny and a domineering spirit. There is no one but Christ who can concentrate in Himself all power, because He is God and because His most perfect humanity is free from all tendency towards sin. None of His representatives on earth would be able without danger to assume at one and the same time His kingship and His priesthood. Out of consideration for their weakness and in order not to expose them to temptation, He has therefore entrusted to two categories of Ministers, priests and kings, the august function of ruling their fellow-men.

We may compare these sage reflexions with another theory of the Fathers of the Church on the origin of the political power, a theory of which we find a curious echo in the eleventh century above the signature of Pope Gregory VII (1080).[7]

> Who does not know [writes the Pope to Bishop Hermann of Metz] that kings and temporal princes had as their ancestors men who, ignoring God, endeavoured with blind passion and intolerable presumption to domineer over their equals, that is, other men, by means of pride, rapine, treachery, murder, in fact by an infinity of criminal acts, very probably instigated by the Prince of this world, the devil?

From these words, which are certainly most unflattering to earthly potentates, the conclusion has somewhat hastily been drawn that, in the eyes of Gregory VII, St. Gregory the Great and St. Augustine, civil authority is a mere product of sin, an effect of diabolical activity. Their real view is more subtle than that. For the Fathers of the Church, indeed, political society is good in itself, it is the lawful outcome of tendencies deeply rooted in human nature: all are agreed on that point. But original sin and its consequences have had the effect of radically corrupting the normal relations of masters and servants, of political authority and its subjects. On the one hand, force has become necessary to subdue disobedient and

rebellious subjects whilst, on the other hand, authority itself—
led astray in its turn by similar deeply-rooted passions—has
tended to be oppressive and tyrannical. The governments of
pagan States which have not learned moderation from any
spiritual power are necessarily affected by this despotic trend,
a fatal consequence of sin.

In regenerated humankind, St. Gelasius sees at work the
medicine brought by Christ to cure this radical evil. "He has
divided the functions of the two powers, assigning to each one
its proper task and dignity." This division of sovereignty is a
permanent antidote against every tyrannical will. Thanks to it,
authority has to become again what it was before the fall: no
longer a brutal and selfish domination, but a service rendered
for the sake of the common good. "You know," said Our Lord,
"that amongst the Gentiles those who claim to bear rule lord
it over them, and those who are great among them make the
most of the power they have. With you it must be otherwise;
whoever has a mind to be great among you must be your
servant, and whoever has a mind to be first among you must
be your slave."[8] In the Christian Society, the State no doubt
retains the right to make use of force and the means of punishment, but the Church, also with sovereign rights, imposes
limits to State domination. She recalls to the State, when need
be, that rule over souls is not within its competence, that unjust
violence transgresses the Divine Law. The Church on her side
regards her mission as being confined to the spiritual domain;
she has neither the direct right of using physical force, nor the
power of subjugating her partner or of making the State into
her docile instrument.

As well as being a remedy against arbitrary despotism, the
dual sovereignty is also a guarantee of spiritual liberty.
Although it be the guardian of public order and of external
morality, the State authority has not the right to impose a
creed. The Church, on the other hand, whilst governing men's
souls and authoritatively setting her doctrine before them, has
not at her disposal, for this purpose, any material force, any
political means of pressure. The human person is therefore not
at the mercy of a single sovereign power which imposes upon
him simultaneously and absolutely a temporal order and a

religious doctrine. He retains, in fact, that fundamental liberty without which neither personal dignity nor true religion could exist for him. The act of faith, in particular, cannot be extorted by force, it must, on pain of being judged valueless, from the moral and from the religious point of view, be perfectly free. This dualism of the spiritual and the temporal normally assures such freedom of conscience, because that physical force which only the State is privileged to employ is properly made use of only in case of attempts against the public peace or against social order.

What matter, then, if the co-existence of Church and State has given rise throughout history to many a dramatic conflict and many a fierce storm? What matter if it has introduced yet further complications into international life? For these trials and practical difficulties are assuredly as nothing in comparison with the decisive part which the dualist system has played and will continue to play in ensuring the protection of the human person and the preservation of his essential liberties.

We shall find indeed, if we consult history, that every grave disturbance of the balance between the two sovereignties inevitably leads to one form of despotism or another. At the close of antiquity the Caesaro-papism of Justinian led to the subjection of the Empire to a crushing tyranny, the effect of which was to set East and West by the ears and finally to destroy that very religious unity which it tried to restore by force. In the Middle Ages it is no mere coincidence that the zenith of the political power of the Papacy should have coincided pretty closely with the foundation of the Inquisition. For, once the secular power was regarded as no more than an instrument of the Church, the temptation to make use of the weapons of temporal punishment in the fight against religious error was bound to be strong. Such measures can doubtless be explained by the state of men's minds in those days, by the alarm resulting from the ravages of the Albigensian heresy, by the very structure (as we shall see later) of medieval civilization; but the fact admittedly remains that they brought with them a serious danger of oppression. In the modern epoch, the renewed preponderance of the State has only too often threatened the liberty of the subject. In England Henry VIII built up a bloody dictatorship on the ruins of the spiritual power and, at the same period, the German princes who had been placed by the Reformation at the head of the churches exercised an intolerable tyranny over men's souls.[9] Let us remember too what the tribunal of the Inquisition became beneath the aegis of the Spanish sovereigns.[10] Closer to our own time the periods of fanatical religious strife in France— the Revolution and later the Combes period—have always been marked by waves of arbitrary violence and tyranny. Finally we know what happened to European liberty beneath the domination of Nazi Germany. So true is it that, bereft of the moderating influence of spiritual sovereignty, the State tends, as though by instinct, towards the most brutal forms of pagan absolutism.

*  *  *

Unstable but necessary: such would appear to an attentive observer to be the epithets most fitted to the dualism of Church and State sovereignty. The fact of this necessity should not however console us too easily for the past and present conflicts between the two sovereignties. We shall speak later about the agreements and contacts which are essential to any positive co-operation between Church and State. For the moment it will suffice if we recall some of the conditions required to enable them to co-exist in peace.

One of these conditions springs at once to mind as an obvious corollary to our preceding remarks: the two sovereignties must mutually recognize their *relative* character and frankly accept the logical consequences.

When, during the medieval period, under the pretext of ensuring Christian unity, certain theologians tended to make of the civil power a simple delegation of the spiritual power, they were laying the foundations of a clerical absolutism which no State worthy of the name could accept. Again, when in the modern period certain doctrinaires in political science refuse to allow that secular sovereignty is subject to any control, any limit, even to any moral law, they are preparing the way, whether they know it or not, for religious war and persecution.

M. G. Renard has well described this state of mind, as it was to be met with in legal circles in about the year 1900:

> For our masters, sovereignty meant absolute power: a power which allows of no restriction, no competition, at least within the territorial frontiers by which it is confined; a relative sovereignty would not be regarded by them as sovereignty; for them, sovereignty and relativity are contradictory terms and therefore two sovereignties cannot be exercised over the same subjects and within the same territories—such is the dogma.[11]

It is in the name of this "dogma" that the Governments of Combes and of Waldeck-Rousseau claimed the right to do away with the Orders within the Church and that they secured —in how fanatical a spirit!—the passing of the Law of Separation.

Owing to a remarkable revulsion of feeling, we have, as already remarked, lived to see in our own days signs of hostile reaction to the absolute State. The power of the State, we hear it said, is not limited only by International Law; within the nation itself its absolute pre-eminence is a highly debatable matter. The State is not the nation and must not be identified with it; it is only a department in the national community. It has thus to reckon with those social, economic, religious and family communities, the rights and the existence of which are by no means dependent on its good pleasure. Even if the State has a right of control over them, even if it does enjoy, unlike any other power, a right to employ physical constraint, it is not within its power either to destroy or to absorb them. These highly suggestive and widely shared opinions are of capital importance in the present connexion, for they place in a clear light the relative character of all earthly authority and they may be expected to influence men's minds in the direction of wide and conciliatory solutions.

In order that the co-existence of Church and State may remain undisturbed, another condition is essential—the difference in order and in nature between the two societies must be clearly recognized. Certain people—and they are numerous—are unable to picture any human society except in terms of a political association. There exists in their minds, one may say, a kind of complex which for them transforms any active and organized collective body into a political party. Our internal struggles are the reason for this; they have left their mark everywhere. As a result of this prejudice, the Catholic Church, with her elaborate organization and her hierarchy, becomes a State within the State, of the same order and on the same plane. Between two such antagonists, all idea of any serious agreement is but a delusion, an obvious impossibility.

In reality these two "perfect societies"—to borrow the language of St. Thomas and of recent Popes—can live together precisely because they do not belong to the same world, to the same human order.

> The Faith teaches us [wrote Pius IX[12]] and human reason demonstrates, that a double order of things exists and that we must therefore distinguish between two earthly powers, the one of natural origin which provides for secular affairs and the tranquillity of human society; the other, of supernatural origin, which presides over the City of God, that is to say the Church of Christ, and which has been divinely instituted for the sake of souls and eternal salvation.

The Church is, then, a spiritual and supernatural society directly ordained for the eternal salvation of its members. The State, on the contrary, is a human and natural society, directly ordained for the temporal good of all. It would be hard to imagine, as between two societies, more radical differences in order, in purpose and consequently in means. Yet it may be objected that, in fact, any distinction of this kind, based on the diverse origin of the two societies, is purely theoretical. The supernatural order is in fact the order under which human nature finds itself living; the state of pure nature, in a world in which Christ would not have become incarnate, is only an abstraction. It is true that the elevation of human nature to the supernatural order has transformed it interiorly in a fashion which makes it impossible for us to divide it into its component parts. There is not in man a nature to which grace could, so to speak, be super-added. Strictly speaking, however, a distinction can be drawn between the elements which constitute our supernaturalized nature—grace is not nature, however intimate their union may be—and this distinction is normally made evident by a differentiation of laws, rights, functions and institutions.

There are political societies which arise spontaneously from the actual requirements of human nature and its social needs, and there is a supernatural community founded by Christ to promote on earth the Kingdom of God. It will moreover be readily admitted that, whatever discussions may take place at the present time in regard to natural law, its content and its juridical character, there exists in earthly societies a human law whose intrinsic connexion with Revelation scarcely permits of demonstration. That Christianity has aided the progress of legal science, that it has enabled men to see legal problems in a clearer light is indeed a conviction shared by many, and this striking fact helps us to realize better the perspicacity of the mind when enlightened by faith; but it would not be safe to deduce from it that the existing law originated from any source other than human reason and social experience. Over against this law of human origin, we have the gospel precepts, our knowledge of which is derived solely from the teachings of the Son of God. Indeed, just as the State's purpose is to lead on human society, by means of human law, to its terrestrial and temporal goal, so the Church has received a mission to guide the faithful towards their eternal destination by means of her own discipline, imbued as it is with the precepts of Christ.

This distinction between the natural and the supernatural order—the essential basis of relations between the Church and State—has been strongly emphasized by recent Popes. Pius XI recalls that there is a natural law, "inscribed by the hand of the Creator Himself on the tablets of the human heart, and that sane reason can read it there when not blinded by sin and passion."[13] It is this law which really lies at the root of all positive law, and in fact harmonizes with the character and aims of the State, these—as Pius XI again remarks—being "not only physical and material but *per se* necessarily comprised within the frontiers of the natural, the terrestrial and the temporal."[14] Before his accession, Pius XII wrote in 1933 that

"the competence of the State is limited to the natural order."[15]
He returns to the subject in his first Encyclical, in which he
declares that the common good, which the State is bound to
further, does not find its essential expression in the material
prosperity of society but, much more, in the "harmonious
development and natural perfection of man for whom the
Creator destined society as a means."[16]

We can well understand the determination of the Popes to
place the sovereignty of the State on a human plane, distinct
from that of the Church, for on the recognition of this fact
depends the maintenance of peace between the spiritual and
temporal elements.

It would, then, be a grave error to advocate a "Christian
State" in the sense of assigning to it the functions and the
duties which are proper to the Church and to the hierarchy.
The civil power is not directly concerned with men's conversion,
with their instruction in the saving truths, with measures to
ensure that they carry out their religious duties. Even though a
revival of religion may take place in a nation, on however large
a scale, the public authorities are precluded as such from
playing any but an indirect part in furthering it. However
profoundly Christian a nation's representatives may be, it is
not for them, in their capacity as heads of the government, to go
outside their secular functions. Their political task ceases on
the threshold of the spiritual domain; it is however concerned
with creating in a nation conditions of material life, of culture,
of civic union, of social justice and public morality such as will
enable the supernatural work of the Church to be freely
developed. We may note in this connexion the moderation
of the requirements which recent Popes lay upon the State.
In the Encyclical *Divini Redemptoris* which he issued in 1937
against Communism, Pope Pius XI called upon the State to
put a stop to atheist propaganda, pointing out that this duty
was laid upon it both by natural law and by the common
belief of mankind; he exhorted Governments to provide for
the welfare of the whole community, and especially for that of
the working classes, by means of wise and far-seeing measures;
and finally he demanded that full opportunity should be
allowed by each nation to the Church for the fulfilment of her

spiritual mission. None of these duties oversteps the natural ends of the State.

It is true that in his Encyclicals on Peace (1922) and on the Kingship of Christ (1925) the same Pope called upon the peoples to recognize the sovereignty of Christ. We must ask ourselves, however, what this recognition of sovereignty actually involves.

> Jesus Christ reigns in civil society [says the Encyclical] when—rendering supreme homage to God—that society recognizes that it is from Him that all authority springs, and derives its rights, this fact being precisely what gives authority its sanction and obedience its imperative character and its sublimity; also when civil society recognizes in the Church those privileges, which it received from its Founder, as being a perfect society, mistress and guide of all other societies; not that it is the Church's wish to diminish the authority of these societies—each of them legitimate within its own sphere—but that she admirably completes them, as grace completes nature.

According to the above Papal teaching, heads of State must admit in the first place that all their power springs from God, that is to say, from Christ, from whom all sovereignty in this world derives. This requirement normally involves a duty on the part of the temporal authorities to be present at certain of the more solemn acts of Christian worship. Civil society thereby expresses, through the presence of its representatives and its deference to the Church, the homage which it owes to God, its Author. It is of course obvious that such participation in Divine worship by the State authorities will be much more marked in a thoroughly Catholic or Christian country than in one where religious allegiance is divided. What more, we may ask ourselves, does such recognition by the State of the universal Kingship of Christ involve? The duty, Pius XI informs us, to respect in practice the independence of the Church, her character as a "perfect society" and her spiritual predominance. Thus we keep on coming back to the same leading principles—The Christian State is not intended to provide directly for the eternal salvation of its citizens: it is not meant to control their religious practices; but it *is* bound to organize social and economic life in a manner which will enable the Church's action to find full scope.

Were the State to lay aside its secular attributes, it would either come into conflict with the Church or else would lose its own independence. But we must be careful not to under-estimate the extent of its sovereignty. In its relations with the spiritual power, the State is not a mere auxiliary charged with material tasks, a kind of plumber called in to carry out some technical adjustments. No, although the human order represented by the State does consist largely of material and economic endeavour, it also includes moral and cultural activities. In this last field, it is true, the State's activity is, as it were, extended by that of the Church in her capacity as guardian of the highest moral and religious values. This does not mean, however, that the secular authority is suppressed or absorbed by the supernatural organization. Revelation has not abrogated natural wisdom in so far as this is productive of law, customs, culture and general principles of morality. All such aspects of civilization on the temporal plane are within the State's competence, no less than is the technical organiza-tion of the national life.

So it is that the Popes have explicitly recognized these privileges of the secular authority. Thus, whilst making all necessary reserves in favour of the Church's superior rights, they loyally admit the important mission which temporal sovereignty has to fulfil within its own sphere. The Liberal notion of the State as "watchdog" has never won their approval. On the contrary, Pius XI, in his Encyclical *Quadragesimo Anno* (1931), praised Leo XIII for "having boldly set aside the barriers within which Liberalism had confined the right of the public authority to intervene", and recommended the said authority to take active steps to organize social justice. Again, Pius XI, in his Encyclical on Education (1929), stated that, in virtue of the same moral mission, State control should extend to the institution of marriage and to the education of children. Such control is no doubt overshadowed by the *magisterium* and supreme jurisdiction of the Church, but what we see here is no mere delegation of spiritual power but something that corresponds to the normal requirements of a political society.

The greatest admiration is due to recent Popes for their constant preoccupation with the need for according full validity, within its own sphere, to secular sovereignty. The same desire for peace and pursuit of a "good neighbour policy" has also made them respect the frontiers of the spiritual domain. The *magisterium* of the Church has certainly never been more active or widely exercised; it deals with all the great problems of religious and moral life, not excepting its social and political aspects. Again, the Church's jurisdiction has never been more powerfully exercised or more dutifully obeyed. Yet there has never been a time when the Church has shown herself more reluctant to commit herself in regard to modes of action that are purely temporal. The rules which have been drawn up, in various countries, for the guidance of Catholic Action well bring out this wise and prudent attitude. True, it is recommended to Catholics, in their capacity as citizens, to make every effort to participate in social and political life but the greatest discretion is enjoined upon them when, as members of Catholic Action, they are entrusted with the task either of aiding, or preparing the way for, the hierarchy's activities. In the first instance, the Catholic citizen, whilst taking for his guiding light the common teaching of the Church, compromises no one but himself and must be prepared to assume, on the temporal plane, his own initiative and his own responsibilities. In the second instance, every active member of Catholic Action must recall that he is speaking for the Church and that there might be a danger of compromising her if any rash decisions were taken in matters political. The contemporary Papacy, therefore, does all within its power to maintain on distinct planes the separate missions of the two powers, thereby obviating, so far as in her lies, the possibilities of conflict.

## *NOTES TO CHAPTER II*

[1] S. Thomas Aquinas, *de Regimine Principum*, I, 14.
[2] Suarez, *de Legibus*, IV, 2;  *Opera Omnia* (edition Vivès), V, pp. 331–333.
By the same Author: *Defensio Fidei*, III, 9; XXIV, p. 249.

3 Matt. xxviii. 20.
4 M. Hauriou, *La Science Sociale Traditionelle*, Paris, 1896, p. 370.
5 L. Le Fur, *Les Grands Problèmes du Droit*, Paris, 1937, p. 228.
6 *De Anathemis Vinculo*, 4. Migne, *Patrol. Lat.*, LIX, 108–109.
7 Register of Gregory VII–VIII, 21 : edition Caspar (Berlin, 1923), pp.552–553. Cf. St. Augustine, *De Doctrina Christiana*, I, 23; *De Civitate Dei*, XIX, 15.
8 Mark x. 42–43.
9 N. Paulus, *Protestantismus und Toleranz im 16 Jahrhundert*, Freiburg-im-Breisgau, 1911, *passim*.
10 J. Lecler, *Le Saint-Siège et l'Inquisition espagnole* in *Recherches de Science Religieuse*, 1935, pp. 45–69.
11 G. Renard, *art.cit.*, pp.8–9.
12 Encyclical *Etsi multa luctuosa* (1873), see Denziger, *Enchiridion Symbolorum*, No. 1841.
13 Encyclical *Mit brennender Sorge* (14 March, 1937).
14 Encyclical *Non abbiamo bisogno* (29 June, 1931).
15 Letter to M. Duthoit (12 July, 1933) in the collection *Action Catholique*, p. 505.
16 Encyclical *Summi Pontificatus* (20 October, 1939).

# III

# AGREEMENT BETWEEN CHURCH AND STATE

WHEN Our Lord distinguished between the civil and the spiritual power He clearly did not mean to imply their radical separation. To distinguish between two things is not the same as to separate them. To ensure that what was Caesar's should be rendered to Caesar and what was God's to God, about the last thing required was a rupture between the Empire of Caesar and the Kingdom of God. As things turned out, however, the Church was forced—from the time of Nero to that of Constantine—to resign herself to living in a state of enmity with, and of separation from, the State. From a providential viewpoint, this state of affairs was, as we have seen, not without its advantages; it allowed the spiritual power to preserve its independence and to avoid being swallowed up in the State. The heads of the Church, however, never regarded this position as normal and definite. In their eyes the two great powers of this world were intended, not to ignore or to fight each other, but to work together for the general benefit of humanity.

This desire for agreement is perceptible from the beginning and made itself felt even when the worst persecutions were at their height. Rare indeed are the writers who, like St. Hippolytus —at the beginning of the third century—describe the Roman empire as "the organ of Antichrist".[1] Faithful to the instructions of St. Peter and St. Paul, the great majority of the Fathers and apologists profess a dutiful loyalty towards the political authorities. St. Irenaeus and Origen recall that it is not the devil but God Himself who has organized the kingdoms of this world.[2] Prayers for the Emperor and for the public authorities were commonly recited during the liturgical assemblies, in accordance with the recommendation of St. Paul.[3] We find a magnificent expression of this attitude, towards the end of the first century, in the Epistle of St. Clement of Rome.[4]

> To our princes, to those who govern us, it is Thou, O Lord, who hast given the power and the royalty, by the magnificent and unfailing virtue of Thy Power, in order that, knowing the glory and the honour which Thou hast bestowed upon them, we may be submissive to them and may not rebel against Thy Will. Grant them, O Lord, peace, concord and stability in order that they may freely exercise the authority which Thou hast conferred upon them. For it is Thou, O Heavenly Master, who givest to the sons of men glory, honour and power over the things of this earth. Direct, O Lord, their counsels in accordance with all that is good, all that is agreeable in Thine eyes, in order that, wielding peaceably and with gentleness the power which Thou hast given them, they may obtain Thy mercy.

The apologists point out in addition that, faithful to Christ's precept, Christians are the first to pay taxes[5] and to fulfil their civic duties. It is true that for rather a long time they remained aloof from public affairs, administrative functions and even from a large number of professions;[6] but the reason for such abstention is to be sought in a complex state of society in which idolatrous rites were closely intertwined with civic and professional life. This rigorous attitude was, moreover, modified as Christianity began to permeate into all classes of society.

The Church, even in the midst of the persecutions, did not confine herself, where the Empire was concerned, to tangible proofs of esteem and goodwill such as those mentioned above. During the same period one can find, in the writings of various ecclesiastics, definite offers of agreement and collaboration. Under the reign of Marcus Aurelius, Meliton of Sardis wrote in his apologia to the Emperor:[7]

> The philosophy which is ours flourished first in barbarian lands; then it spread abroad amongst the nations during the great reign of Augustus, thine ancestor, and it has been

of good omen, particularly for thine own reign. It is from this moment indeed that one must date the grandiose development of the Roman power of which thou, with thy son, wilt be the heir acclaimed by our troth, if thou wilt but allow life to this philosophy which, contemporary with Augustus, has been in some sense the foster-sister of the Empire and which thine ancestors have respected together with the other religions. A proof that this philosophy of ours is destined to share the Empire's prosperity may be found in the fact that since Augustus's day thou hast experienced no defeat and hast, on the contrary, reaped in every thing all the success and glory that thy heart could desire.

Origen in like manner was to represent the Church—in his Treatise against Celsus (about 250)—as the natural ally of the Empire, on the grounds that the *Pax Romana* had providentially facilitated the rapid diffusion of the Gospel.[8]

Such an attitude on the part of primitive Christianity towards a persecuting State is most remarkable, and bears witness to a desire for understanding which has since then crystallized into a solid tradition. The Church cannot of course link up her cause irrevocably with any particular temporal régime; she has other interests to defend than those that are purely terrestrial in character. Nevertheless, so far as the circumstances of the time permit, she seeks to work in harmony with the existing State authorities. Just as after the Peace of Milan and the conversion of Constantine she had been the ally of the Empire, so when the Roman power collapsed she adopted a friendly attitude to the barbarian kingships. This attitude was not due to any naïve opportunism on the Church's part but to her desire to further the common good, both spiritual and temporal.

The contemporary Papacy is thus remaining faithful to the constant practice of the Church when, repudiating the principle of separation, it so forcefully advocates a policy of agreement between the two powers. From amongst a multitude of similar utterances we may choose for quotation the words of Leo XIII, in the Encyclical *Arcanum*, on Christian marriage:

> This agreement and harmony (which should reign between Church and State) is not only best for the two powers, but

is the most opportune and efficient means of securing
through their joint efforts—the welfare of the human race
all that regards temporal life and the hope of etern
salvation. When the civil authority comes to a friend
understanding with the Church, such an agreement neces
arily procures great advantages for both powers, just a
when the human intellect embraces the Christian religion
it is greatly ennobled and becomes far more capable o
avoiding and fighting error, whilst faith for its part receives
valuable assistance from the intellect. The dignity of the
State is in fact enhanced and, seeing that it is guided by
religion, the government always remains just. At the same
time this harmony between the two powers procures for the
Church defensive and protective aid which is to the advantage
of the faithful.

★       ★       ★

In this pregnant passage Leo XIII does not merely recom-
mend in general terms a harmonious relationship between the
two powers, he emphasizes the grave reasons which can be
adduced in favour of such harmony. On many grounds the
loyal collaboration of Church and State can indeed be shown
to be not only desirable but essential.

In the first place the true end of the State is closely bound
up with spiritual aims. For, although distinct in their origin,
in their nature and in the immediate term of their activities,
the two societies have none the less in view the same ultimate
goal which is that of the whole human community, the eternal
salvation of all its members. The Church tends directly towards this goal by means of all her beliefs, rites and discipline.
The State, for its part, whilst having the same end in view, must
do so indirectly. It does not, strictly speaking, carry out any
religious duty, but it must so order its government and temporal administration that the action of the Church may be
facilitated, and that no obstacle may impede the members of
the State in their spiritual liberty. Such co-ordination can only
be achieved in an atmosphere of unity and reciprocal understanding. How indeed could two independent powers combine
for the same purpose, each in its own sphere, without mutual
contracts and a certain amount of give and take? The above

considerations make it easier for us to understand why recent Popes have so vigorously denounced the complete laicization of the State. The doctrines of the lay State are repugnant to the Church; they make any understanding with the spiritual power impossible; they imprison the State so completely in its temporal functions that it no longer concerns itself with God or with the Church, or even with the spiritual needs of its own subjects. "As for the pretensions", wrote Leo XIII, "of those who would make the State completely extraneous to religion and who hold that it can administer public affairs without taking any more account of God than it would if He did not exist, we have here a temerity unexampled even among pagans."9

It is precisely because she recognizes the independence of the State in its own sphere that the Church seeks for its co-operation for the common good of humanity. Between autonomous powers such a harmonization of aims cannot be achieved by rigorous and, so to speak, mechanical means; it must be brought about by means of a constant interplay of mutual sympathy as well as through friendly agreements.

This understanding is rendered all the more necessary by the fact that the political power and the spiritual power have identical interests in certain domains. In order to decide in the best way possible the problem of their respective competences, it is not enough simply to say: "Temporal matters are the affairs of the State, spiritual matters of the Church." First of all we must define what we mean by "temporal". Some, as we have seen, would like to limit the temporal power to purely technical and material concerns, the Church having complete control over all moral and religious life. This would no doubt provide a convenient method of establishing between the two powers an exactly defined frontier; but such a view seems to us indefensible, for the direct competence of the State extends to law, justice and morality, in so far as these disciplines derive from natural wisdom and from reason. Now, it is precisely on this moral and juridical plane that Church and State meet and that they risk clashing. There are then in the life of a nation many "mixed questions" which only general principles can resolve.

The Popes have thrown a clear light upon the existence of "mixed problems" which do not fall exclusively within the Church's competence. Leo XIII, for instance, has noted this to be the case—where marriage is concerned—in his Encyclical *Arcanum* (1880):

> The Church is not unaware that the Sacrament of Marriage, which also has for its object the maintenance and increase of human society, has necessary connexions and relationships with human interests resulting from marriage but appertaining to the civil order; and these things belong quite properly to the competence, and fall within the scope, of those who are at the head of the State.

Again, in the matter of the education of children, the same fact is recognized by Pius XI in the special Encyclical which he issued on the subject in 1929:

> No injury to the authentic and personal rights of the State can result from the primordial rights of the Church and the family in matters of education. These rights are bestowed upon civil society by the Author of Nature Himself, not in virtue of any right of fatherhood, such as is claimed by the Church and the family, but for the sake of the authority without which the State cannot promote the common good which is indeed its true end.[10]

Education and teaching, marriage and the institution of the family, ecclesiastical and monastic patrimonies, clerical immunities, religious association . . . in all these complex questions we find that the spiritual and temporal powers are simultaneously concerned. It is consequently impossible to draw a hard and fast line between the spheres of action proper to each authority.

In such conditions the absolute separation of Church and State, so contrary to traditional doctrine, must either be an illusion or else a challenge to common sense. It is as though two administrations were to pretend to be unaware of each other's existence in spite of the fact that multiple causes of friction existed between them! Far from leading to peace, such a state of affairs would mean a chronic state of cold war and, as a result, the oppression of the weak by the strong. This point

was made long ago by Pius X, in the course of his condemnation of the Law of Separation:[11]

Since the two societies have the same subjects, over which
each within its own sphere wields authority, it is yet necessarily
a fact that there are many matters which it is essential for
both societies to know as coming within the competence of
both. Now, once agreement between Church and State has
disappeared, these matters of common concern will become
the breeding ground of numerous differences which will
become very acute on both sides.

Church and State cannot ignore one another without
harming one another: this is the basic reason which has always
led the Popes to reject the separation principle. There is
therefore only one normal means whereby they can resolve
any disputes that may arise; this is the method employed by
secular sovereignties in order to settle their differences peacefully: the two parties must keep in contact, must negotiate and
must conclude agreements.

There are two Powers [wrote Leo XIII in the Encyclical
*Nobilissima Gallorum* (1884)] both subject to a natural and
eternal law and responsible, each within its own sphere, for
the things made subject to their sway. But, whenever it is
a matter of settling anything which, owing to various rights,
and also on various grounds, interests the two powers, the
public good demands and exacts, that an agreement be
established between them . . . It is for this reason that,
when an order of things has been publicly established by
means of conventions between the ecclesiastical power and
the civil power, the public interest—no less than equity—
demands that the agreement remain inviolate, for if mutual
services are rendered by both sides, both also benefit by
them.

These last remarks by Leo XIII are of a nature to encourage
us to examine more closely the advantages which mutual
friendly relations can afford both to Church and State. These
relations are not entirely analogous to those of two governments
which are drawn together by a common desire for peace. The
fact that the powers of this world have clearly demarcated

territories of their own greatly diminishes the likei hood of any
one of them obtaining ascendancy over the internal politics of
its neighbour. The same does not apply to the relations between
the Church and secular sovereignties but, although the identity
of territory and of subjects doubtless increases the risk of
conflict, it also is favourable to the exercise of salutary influences
for, to put the whole thing in a nutshell, the Church and the
State have need of one another to accomplish—in normal
fashion—their respective missions.

The Church can count on Our Lord's aid in the midst of
the gravest peril; she fears, therefore, neither war nor persecution. She has clearly demonstrated, in the course of her history,
that even the greatest political and social upheavals are powerless to prevent her from continuing her work and pursuing her
mission. It is none the less true that a peaceful atmosphere is
greatly to her advantage; she needs it in order to consolidate
her conquests and to expand her organization. In very early
days St. Paul is found recommending the faithful to pray for
kings and governments "in order that we may lead a peaceful
and quiet life";[12] he realized that the state of peace reigning
throughout the Empire was in its own way a help to the diffusion
of the Gospel. In spite of his reserved attitude towards the
terrestrial city, St. Augustine fully appreciated the value to the
Church of the "peace of Babylon":

> The terrestrial city which does not live by faith seeks for
> terrestrial peace. Such is the aim which it pursues in that
> union of citizens in virtue of which some command, whilst
> others obey. The terrestrial city desires that there should
> prevail amongst them, in regard to all that concerns this
> mortal life, a certain harmony of will—but the celestial city,
> or rather the portion of that city which lives by faith and
> makes its pilgrimage through this mortal life, also needs to
> make use of this earthly peace. Such a peace is, in fact,
> necessary for the members of the city until their mortal
> condition ceases. So long therefore as the Church remains
> captive and passes the time of her exile in the bosom of the
> terrestrial city, she has no hesitation in obeying the laws of
> that city in accordance with which all things are administered
> that are necessary to the support of man in this mortal life;

and since this dying condition is common to all, the Church desires, for the sake of all those things which concern her present interests, to preserve harmony between the two cities.[13]

In order, then, to be able to carry out her religious activities, the Church attaches importance to the aid which civil concord brings her. She knows by experience that any spiritual gains which are hers must remain precarious in a land devastated by war or given over to anarchy. Rightly desirous to make sure that her work will be thorough and lasting, she welcomes with gratitude the co-operation of the civil authorities when these endeavour to produce, within their own sphere, an atmosphere of peace and security.

Nor has the State any less need of the Church if it is to carry out its temporal obligations worthily. The fulfilment of its moral and cultural mission is in fact beyond its unaided powers: it cannot, in practice, achieve its ends without the assistance of the spiritual City:

> When religion is banished from civil society [wrote Pius IX in 1864[14]], when the doctrine and authority of the Divine Revelation are rejected, the true conception of justice and human law becomes obscured, and physical force takes the place of justice and true law.

There lies in this reflexion by a great Pope a grave and disturbing truth. The State left to itself loses the sense of its natural vocation as guardian of law, peace and justice. It becomes, like a man without grace, simply the plaything of its own sinful tendencies: instincts of violence, of despotism, of tyrannical domination. Outside those *milieux* where a Christian atmosphere prevails, we can see, amongst individuals as well as amongst their rulers, that the sense of simple human and moral values, the old respect for the law and for human dignity, the cult of natural justice and equity, are gradually growing blurred. The complete secularization of the State, as present experience shows, seems to involve this terrifying consequence: the "regress" of humanity towards that lapsed state from which Christ came to save us. Strange though this may seem, a sense of justice cannot be maintained except in an atmosphere of charity. Fallen man has grown too feeble to practise of his own accord the virtues proper to his state; he needs an assistance which Christ's grace alone can procure for him. Human society is just as powerless in this respect as the members of which it is composed; the State which administers and represents it will be no better provided for; it will not succeed in being, here below, the instrument of right and of justice unless it can count upon the collaboration and the assistance of the spiritual society.

*      *      *

Whilst, as we have just noted, the union of Church and State is—from so many points of view—a moral necessity, this union can in practice be realized under many very different forms:

> The relations of Church and State [wrote Cardinal Baudrillart[15]] are not regulated in accordance with absolute and, so to speak, geometrical principles; they result from the social and political situation and from the manner in which the Church adapts her principles to meet it.

In the Middle Ages a sort of "customary law" (to use the expression of Hauriou) was accepted alike by the Church and by the temporal sovereignties. It found no precise juridical expression but it was solid and durable, anchored, one may say, in the customs and minds of men. Even when political feeling ran highest, the idea of a divorce between Throne and Altar would have occurred to no one. The quarrels between the representatives of both left intact a traditional alliance. There were at that time no concordats, strictly speaking, but only special conventions of limited range. The celebrated document known by the name of the Concordat of Worms (1122) is less wide in its scope than might be imagined. Concluded between Callixtus II and the Emperor Henry V, in order to put a stop to the Investitures dispute, it only concerns one particular point in ecclesiastical law: episcopal elections and the right of the Emperor to confer upon the Bishop-elect the temporalities of his See. The document does not actually call itself a Concordat but consists of two documents, of almost identical tenor, one of which is entitled "The Emperor's Privilege" and the other "The Privilege of the Sovereign Pontiff". It is none the less worth mentioning as being a celebrated forerunner of the future agreements between the Roman Church and the national States.

The era of the Concordats happens to coincide more or less exactly with that of the rise of the great European nations. In 1448, this time under the name of "Concordat", an important settlement in regard to ecclesiastical benefices was jointly signed by Pope Nicholas V and the Emperor Frederick III, representing the "German Nation". Still more far-reaching in its clauses was the Concordat of Boulogne (1516) between Leo X and Francis I. It abrogated the ill-starred Pragmatic Sanction of Bourges (1438) which Rome had never recognized, and remained in force until the very end of the *ancien régime*. Other agreements of the same kind were later concluded between the Holy See and European States. They multiplied in the eighteenth century and so became the normal formula for agreements between Church and State.

The important series of nineteenth-century Concordats was inaugurated by that of 1801. Concluded between Pius VII and Bonaparte, with a view to the restoration of religion in France after the revolutionary upheaval, it was abolished in 1905 by a unilateral decision on the part of the French Government. Almost all the other States of Europe and Latin America regularized their relations with Rome in the same manner. It was only towards the beginning of the twentieth century that separatist principles triumphed in several countries and notably in France.

The concordatory system is in itself an excellent arrangement: it well emphasizes the sovereignty of the contracting parties and the character of "perfect society" which belongs to the Church as well as to the State. These solemn agreements between the Holy See and national governments enable questions on the border-line between the spiritual and the temporal to be peacefully solved. The reciprocal concessions which they contain make manifest, in a tangible and concrete fashion, the desire of both parties to come to an understanding with each other. The Church, as we may well imagine, is, in principle, altogether favourable to this system.

Nevertheless, these modern Concordats have not been productive only of advantage to the Church. These "agreements" have in many cases proved to be sources of disagreement. This has been due in the first place to the very considerable differences of opinion between jurists and canonists as to the essential character of such conventions. The canonists have been unwilling to admit the contractual character of the Concordats; many of them have seen in them nothing but the simple concession of revocable privileges granted by the Holy See at the demand of a government, the supremacy of the spiritual over the temporal forbidding the Pope (so it has been contended) to commit himself further. The jurists, for their part, have opposed to this view the "legal" theory, according to which the Concordat was simply a law of the State; it had been promulgated no doubt after an understanding with Rome, but the secular authority was always free to revoke it when it chose.[16] Such contradictory principles could not but lead, in practice, to the most regrettable conflicts, and rendered highly precarious the observance of the obligations assumed by both parties.

From the eighteenth century onwards, the position resulting from these divergent interpretations was rendered yet more unsatisfactory, because of the growing absolutism of State sovereignty. Intoxicated by their own omnipotence, modern States have frequently sought to twist the sense of the Concordats in such a way as to transform them, if possible, into instruments of domination. In a singularly illogical manner, as governments grew more secularist and anti-clerical, they forced the hand of the Holy See in order that they themselves might be enabled to retain control of spiritual affairs. One of the most exorbitant of the concessions extorted was that of the nominations of bishops by the temporal power. This dated from the Concordat of 1516 and was revived in that of 1801. The exercise of such a right, which had seemed excessive even when the Most Christian King was concerned, appeared quite intolerable in the hands of an authority which was hostile to the Church or even when it was merely indifferent to religion.

"This right," says Père de la Brière, "then became a pure anachronism, a misconception, an instrument whereby governments attempted to subject the religious authority of each diocese to the purely human and purely secular caprices of the temporal power."[17]

Even worse things occurred. Certain governments thought that they could add to the Concordats—without even consulting the Holy See—a number of police regulations which distorted their whole character. Even under the old régime in France the members of the *Parlement* had codified under the title of "Liberties of the Gallican Church" a series of orders the object of which seems to us perfectly clear, viz. to place the French clergy under the rigorous control of the secular authority. We note that many of these provisions have the effect of placing the spiritual power in shackles; thus, the Papal Legate is forbidden to exercise his authority without the Royal permission (art. 11); the Bishops are forbidden to go to Rome unless the King agrees (art. 13); the Royal *placet* must be obtained for the publication of any Bull emanating from the Holy See (art. 44); the Pope is forbidden to send a direct summons to appear before the Court of Rome to any subject of the King (art. 45); members of Religious Orders are forbidden to ask the Holy See, without the Royal consent, for exemption from the diocesan authority (art. 71) . . . [18] After the Revolution, this precedent was kept in mind. Under the name of *Articles Organiques* the Gallican maxims reappeared in the police regulations annexed to the Concordat of 1801 by the Imperial Government.[19] In this wise, under the shelter of an agreement with Rome and on the pretext of ensuring its execution, the civil power found a means of imposing on the French clergy a most despotic tyranny.

The grave inconveniences of the above kind that are involved in modern Concordats did not have the effect of making the Holy See despair of an understanding with the temporal authorities. It did not weary of the unequal struggle or throw over the Concordat system in favour of the separation of Church and State. What would have been the use? For, as a juridical formula, separation can become, in its turn, a dangerous instrument of oppression.

Thus, the period between the two world wars was marked by profound changes, the object of which was to ensure that concordatory pacts concluded in the future would be more stable in character. Between 1922 and 1935, no less than thirteen Concordats were concluded between Pope Pius XI and various European States. To these we must add the Concordat with Portugal, signed in Rome on the 7th May, 1940, and ratified at Lisbon on the following 1st June.[20] These new agreements contrast strongly with those of the nineteenth century in their essential provisions. Thanks to their number and the repetition of identical clauses, they have created, as it were, a sort of concordatory common law which is much more favourable to spiritual interests. None of them, for example, has retained the old arrangement whereby bishops were nominated by the secular power: this right is reserved to the Holy See after consultation with the Head of the State. All these new Concordats admit that the freedom to practise the Catholic religion involves the recognition by the State of ecclesiastical "moral persons", particularly the Orders and Congregations. All proclaim that the faithful and their pastors shall enjoy complete liberty in their relations with the Sovereign Pontiff; and this liberty of course includes the free publication of ecclesiastical decisions which, according to the old Gallican usage, was subject to the *placet* of the Head of the State. Finally, all of them endeavour, in their different manners, to ensure the agreement of the secular legislature with the recent rulings of Canon Law. What is more, the evolution of legal doctrines has led to the progressive abandonment of the old rival theories, the theory of privilege and the legal theory, which gave a unilateral character to concordatory obligations. Nowadays, Concordats are normally regarded as real pacts, analogous to international conventions and imposing, in justice, mutual obligations on both parties. Père de la Brière admirably sums up present-day opinion when he writes: "Concordats, like all other diplomatic conventions, constitute bilateral agreements between sovereign powers and involve reciprocity of contractual obligations . . . Church and State here treat as between Power and Power and contract synallagmatic obligations in the field of public law and of international law."[21]

If we add that the concordatory common law which results
from the multiplication of the same essential clauses normally
has the effect of excluding arbitrary interpretations and
unjustifiable conclusions, it must be admitted that the Concordats negotiated by Pius XI and Pius XII show a notable
and decided advance upon former agreements of this kind.

Does this mean that, as a result of the improvement noted, an
understanding between the two powers is necessarily of a more
binding character than formerly? It would be rash to commit
oneself to such a view. Certain recent Concordats, particularly
that with the Third Reich, have caused grievous disappointment to the Holy See. Indeed, however admirable and well-
balanced a treaty may be in itself, its real value must always
be completely dependent on the good will of the two contracting
parties; and this reminds us that a state of concord between
the two powers will never find complete expression in official
formulae. We cannot measure the thoroughness of an understanding between the Papacy and any earthly State by the
perfection of the legal instrument which binds them. Pius XI
grasped this point very firmly and expressed it neatly when, in
his allocution *Iam Annus* of the 14th December, 1925, he gave
the following appreciation of the state of affairs resulting from
the separation of Church and State in Chile: "In the light of
the Catholic Faith, this arrangement is certainly not in conformity with the doctrine of the Church . . . However, it is
applied in so benevolent a manner that, far from being a
separation, it is rather a friendly union."[22]

As may be gathered from the above words of Pius XI, the
official position in various countries—whether it be based on
a Concordat or on separation—often fails to reflect with accuracy
the true state of relations between Church and State. The
Concordat arrangement undoubtedly corresponds better in
principle with the Church's ideal; it sets its stamp alike on the
agreement of the two powers and on their respective sovereignty.
The above is only true, however, provided that the Concordat
really is the outward expression of a profound desire for mutual
understanding and esteem. Should this not be the case, all
that we have is a simple document which will carry little weight
with a petty-minded or hostile jurisprudence: it may perhaps,

even so, serve to prevent certain overt acts of aggression, but it will no longer be an instrument of peace and co-operation fitted to set the seal of mutual sympathy upon the relations between Church and State. As regards separation, this too must not be judged solely by external appearances. True separation, harmful separation, resides, not so much in formulae as in the legislator's determination either to ignore the Church or else to discriminate against her. In face of such an attitude as this, the Holy See, as we know, will always remain unyielding. It is possible, however, that, for grave factual reasons and in order to safeguard religious peace in a divided country, there may be legal separation and at the same time a discreet understanding with the Church that action will be taken in agreement with her. This, to borrow the expression of Pius XI, may be called "a friendly union", even though it be devoid of a basis in law. Such is the position of Brazil and of Chile: it is also, we may add, the position of present-day France. The Law of 1905 is still in force; but while, in the mind of its authors, it was an act of hostility directed against the Holy See and the French clergy, it has ended, little as they anticipated this, by transforming itself into a kind of "friendly union"—a consummation peculiarly gratifying to French Catholics.

To sum up, the peaceful co-existence of Church and State requires for its realization a policy of understanding and of cordial relationship. The most important thing of all, if this end is to be attained, is a determined resolve on the part of each to understand the other, to unite, to collaborate in the great work common to both, namely, the promotion of the temporal and spiritual progress of humanity. Without this basic goodwill, without this mutual understanding, the most pompous official agreements are but empty words, or worse, instruments of oppression. When, on the other hand, a sympathy based on reason exists between the two parties, disputes die down and obstacles grow less formidable. The official expression of this basic understanding will be more or less precise, more or less detailed, in accordance with circumstances and the conditions of the countries concerned. It may take the form of a concordat in good and true form, of a more modest *modus vivendi*, of a special arrangement in regard to a disputed question; even,

for grave reasons, of a legal separation. The essential thing is
that there should obtain, between the Holy See and national
governments, a policy of reciprocal contacts which will make
it possible to find a rapid solution for passing difficulties and
to maintain between the two parties a deep and lasting
sentiment of esteem.[23]

## NOTES TO CHAPTER III

[1] Cf. J. Neumann, *Hippolytus von Rom in seiner Stellung zu Staat und Welt*, Leipzig, 1902, p. 58. It is also to be remembered that St. John in the Apocalypse shows no tenderness for the Roman Empire.

[2] Irenaeus, *Adv. Haereses*, V; Migne, *Patrol. Graec.*, VII, 1186. Origen, *in Rom.*, IX, 26; *P.G.*, XIV, 1226–1227.

[3] I Tim. ii. 2.

[4] Clement of Rome, *Ad Corinthios*, 61; edition of Hemmer, p.127. Cf. Tertullian, *Apologetic*, 30–31.

[5] St. Justin, *I Apol.* 17.

[6] Cf. J. Lebreton, in Martin et Fliche, *Histoire de l'Eglise*, Vol. II, Paris, 1935, p. 68.

[7] Meliton, *Apologia*, in Eusebius, *Ecclesiastical History*, IV, 26, 7.

[8] Origen, *Contra Celsum*, II, 30; Migne, *P.G.*, XI, 849.

[9] Encyclical *Humanum Genus*.

[10] Pius XI, Encyclical on *Education*, in *The Acts of Pius XI*, Vol. VI, pp. 106–107.

[11] Encyclical *Vehementer* (1906).

[12] I Tim. ii. 2.

[13] St. Augustine, *De Civitate Dei*, XIX, 17: Migne, *Patrol. Lat.*, XLI, 645.

[14] Encyclical *Quantra Cura*. Denzinger, *Enchiridion*, No. 1691.

[15] Alfred Baudrillart, *Quatre Cents Ans de Concordat*, Paris, 1905, p.14.

[16] H. Wagnon, *Concordats et Droit International*, Gembloux, 1935, pp. 2–6.

[17] Y. de la Brière: *La renaissance de Droit canonique dans plusieurs legislations séculières*, extract from the *Acts of the Congress of International Law* (Rome, 1934), p. 12.

[18] The 83 articles of the Liberties of the Gallican Church by P. Pithou (1594) can be found in the *Manuel du Droit Public et Ecclésiastique* by M. Dupin, Paris, 1880, p. 1–85.

[19] Dupin, *op.cit.*, pp. 199–214.

[20] Y. de la Brière, *Le Droit Concordataire de la nouvelle Europe* (*Extrait des Cours de l'Académie du Droit International*), Paris, 1939. Paul Parsy, *L'Eglise et les Etats: Les Concordats Récents, 1914–1935*, Paris, 1936.

21 Y. de la Brière, *Le Droit Concordataire*, p. 13.
22 *Acta Apostolicae Sedis*, 1925, p. 642.
23 This policy of reciprocal contacts is generally implemented by the appointment of a diplomatic mission, by the presence of official delegates at religious ceremonies and of ecclesiastical representatives at civil solemnities. It is entirely compatible with a state of separation between Church and State—as we may see from the position in France and in some other countries.

# IV

# THE PRIMACY OF THE SPIRITUAL: ITS PRACTICAL EXPRESSION THROUGHOUT THE AGES

THE foregoing deductions from Catholic doctrine—the distinction between the two powers and the need for agreement between them—introduce into our discussion a new and important problem. If Church and State are two "perfect" and sovereign societies, should they treat one another on an equal footing? Must we look upon them as we should upon two powers of this world which, conscious of their own independence, enter into alliances with one another and conclude treaties? The reply is clear: Church and State do not belong to the same order, and the two orders have their fixed hierarchical places. The Church is superior to the State as the spiritual is superior to the temporal, as an institution of supernatural origin takes precedence over an earthly organization, the creature of human nature and of its social needs. In a passage of the Encyclical *Arcanum* (1880), from which a quotation has already been given, Leo XIII strongly emphasizes the relative subordination of the political society:

> As regards questions which are subject to simultaneous assessment by both Cities—even though under different aspects—the City which has to deal with human things is dependent, as is right and proper, on the other City which has received the custody of heavenly things.

If we ask ourselves, however, in what manner this dependence is shown, and what rights are conferred upon the Church by her natural superiority, we find ourselves faced by a grave and complex problem which, even to-day, gives rise to heated discussions. In the purely political field we know what is meant by the existence of bonds of dependence and vassalage between one State and another. It is a sharing out of functions between a subject power and a suzerain power, to which is added—to the latter's advantage—a right of control and of intervention. In that case, however, we are dealing with earthly powers which share rights of the same order: justice, finance, police, administration. What becomes of these relations of subordination when we see facing one another two powers which are heterogeneous and yet hierarchically connected? Must the superior power—in this case the spiritual side—come, if need be, out into the open and, in order to assert its supremacy, assume temporal prerogatives? Again, how can the spiritual power vindicate its claims if it forbids itself all temporal weapons, all specifically secular action? and, supposing it does so, can there be any question, strictly speaking, of the jurisdiction of the Church over the City?

In order to find a solution of difficulties like these, which retain their importance to-day, we can only think of one method which will serve our needs, that of consulting, in history's pages, the actual experiences of the spiritual society. The Church did not come into the world with a ready-made doctrine to govern her relations with the secular powers. She has defined her attitude step by step, in order to cope with situations which grew progressively more complex. Over a period of almost two thousand years she has known every kind of political régime, she has been in contact with the most diverse civilizations, she has experienced, turn by turn, man's favour, his indifference and his hostility. Needless to say, all the Church's acts have not the same significance, the same absolute value. Some of them, whilst easily enough to justify in the circumstances which prompted them, could not be erected, without pressing cause, into rules for all to follow. Any exposition of the Church's doctrine on political matters must then depend upon history; it must show how the Church, placed by her Founder in the living world of temporal civilizations, herself learned wisdom by contact with events and enriched herself from century to century through an ever wider experience of men and things. It is thus that, in the developments of our thesis which are now to follow, light will be thrown on the primacy of the spiritual power, its nature and its essential requirements.

We shall obviously leave out of account the right of the Popes to exercise, over a limited territory, a true temporal jurisdiction. The question of the States of the Church is not within the scope of our discussion. It will be enough at present for us to envisage the rights of the spiritual sovereignty over the nations and powers of this world.

*         *         *

In Christian antiquity the politics of the Church derived from one essential need: that of safeguarding, against the Empire, her own existence and independence. The introduction of the dualist system did not, as we have seen, come about without a struggle or the shedding of blood. Thousands of martyrs died to secure the independence of the spiritual City; and when the era of persecutions had drawn to its close, the Church, in the person of her heads, had to fight in order to save herself from being absorbed into the Empire by the government of the Christian Caesars:

> Let us compare the Imperial dignity to that of the head of the Church [Pope Symmachus wrote, at the beginning of the sixth century, to the Emperor Anastasius[1]]. There is this capital difference between them, that one has the care of earthly things and the other of divine things. Emperor, thou art there to administer human affairs, whilst it is for the Pontiff to dispense to thee the Divine mysteries. *The latter's dignity is surely equal, not to say superior, to thine.* Thou wilt say perhaps that it is written: "Every soul must be submissive to its lawful superiors" (Rom. xiii, 1) . . . This is true; but, if every power comes from God, this must be true *a fortiori* of the power which is set over divine affairs.

This text is highly characteristic. If it strongly emphasizes the dualism of the Empire and of the spiritual society, it insists, on the other hand, but little on the subordination of the

Emperor:"The Pontiff's dignity is surely equal, not to say superior, to thine." The reason is that, at that time, there was as yet scarcely any question of a jurisdiction, strictly speaking, by the Church over things temporal. Let us make no mistake: the intrinsic superiority of the spiritual is not in question. The Church represents *vis-à-vis* the State the rights of conscience, and these are expressed in the Apostolic phrase: "It is better to obey God than man . . . "[2] In later years the Fathers of the Church were wont to dwell, under different symbols, on the difference in nature between the two powers. Thus they compared their relationship to that between heaven and earth, between body and soul, between gold and lead. From none of these comparisons, however—not even from that of body and soul—did they deduce any right by the Church to temporal jurisdiction. It was left for the Middle Ages to push such symbolism to its extreme limit and to justify, by its means, the bold interventions of the Church in the secular field.

Much stress was laid in the medieval period on two quotations, one from St. Augustine and one from Pope St. Gregory, in which the Imperial dignity seems to be presented as an office or function of the Church. St. Augustine expressed his idea in the form of a wish: "How blessed the Emperors would be if they placed their might at the service of the Divine Majesty with a view to the spread of Christianity!"[3] St. Gregory was more categoric when he said in a letter of 593 A.D. to the Byzantine Emperor: "Power over all men has been given to my Lords that they may throw open more widely the way that leads to Heaven, in order that the earthly Kingdom may be at the service of the heavenly Kingdom."[4] In practice, the demands made on the State both by the Bishop of Hippo and by Gregory the Great were very modest: so much so that the latter has been reproached for adopting an unduly complacent attitude towards the Imperial authority.

Christian antiquity at any rate handed on to later epochs one memorable precedent, that of the excommunication of the Emperor Theodosius. The reason for this is well known; in order to crush a revolt in the city of Thessalonica, the Emperor had the populace put to the sword. Against this criminal exertion of authority, St. Ambrose of Milan reacted with energy, pronouncing against the guilty ruler a sentence of excommunication. This was the first world-famous inter-vention—*ratione peccati*—of a great ecclesiastical leader in temporal affairs. Be it noted, however, that, in this celebrated case, the spiritual power did not trespass outside its own province. All it did was to promulgate, and that by means of secret missives, an ecclesiastical penalty. Theodosius gave way and, after a certain period of exclusion from the Church, he was absolved on Christmas day and readmitted to the ranks of the faithful.

*    *    *

The break-up of the Roman Empire meant the inauguration of an entirely new period, so far as the Church was concerned, for the primacy of the spiritual would now, in progressive stages, begin to find its expression through the exercise of jurisdiction over things temporal. In order that we may justly appreciate this transformation we must recall the exceptional circumstances which occasioned or even necessitated the change.

To read certain historical works one would imagine that the policy of the great Popes of the Middle Ages was the result of the evolution of doctrine, the effect of theological speculation on the various concepts of St. Gregory or St. Augustine. Far be it from us to minimize the importance, in relation to our subject, of this slow but steady doctrinal evolution; but we must not, even so, lose sight of the altogether exceptional conditions in which the Church and, with her, Western Civilization found themselves placed at this time.

Once the Roman Empire had disappeared, all culture, whether legal, political, literary or philosophic, disintegrated rapidly, so far as the laity were concerned. It is indeed no exaggeration to say that, between the sixth and the end of the eleventh century, all independent lay culture disappeared from the West. Outside clerical and monastic circles, with very few exceptions, intellectual activities were at a standstill; the study of political problems and of questions of public interest were abandoned. Thus, in a new world, in which the barbarian elements were fusing gradually with the ancient populations of Europe, the Church, without having sought the position for herself, found herself, for several centuries, the sole guardian of the treasures of civilization. Laymen knew how to fight but, with the rarest exceptions, they did not know how to write or to think. "Until the twelfth century," M. Schnürer has pointed out, "the Church and its representatives were the sole trustees of those intellectual forces which upheld the sovereign in his policy and in his government of the State. It was almost exclusively amongst the clergy too that men could be found who were capable of drawing up acts and decrees and of engaging in scientific and artistic labours."[5]

The consequences of this state of affairs can easily be imagined. In antiquity Church and Empire formed two distinct entities between which no compromise was possible. Even after it had become Christian and before its laws and legislature had become penetrated by Christian influences, the Empire remained a secular organization which did not owe to the Faith of Christ either its origin or its constituent elements. In the Frankish epoch, on the other hand, the barbarian monarchies could not manage without the Church, the only organized power in which, together with intellectual culture, some notion of the *res publica* survived together, with some political knowledge. An eminent personality like Charlemagne succeeded in dominating western Christianity for a time, his prestige eclipsing that of the Papacy itself, but Charlemagne drew his principal advisers entirely from the clergy, he lived and thought in an exclusively ecclesiastical atmosphere; his "capitularies" and his admonitions bore the most startling resemblance to the Canons of Councils and the sermons of preachers. The following is an example of the kind of language employed by the *Missi Dominici*, the inspectors and representatives of the sovereign, when addressing themselves to the populace:

Listen, Beloved Brethren, to the warning which our Master the Emperor Charles addresses to you by our lips. We are sent here for the sake of your salvation, and we are instructed to warn you to live virtuously in accordance with God's law and justly in accordance with the law of this world. We bid you to know in the first place that you must believe in One God, Father, Son and Holy Ghost. Love God with all your heart. Love your neighbour as yourselves, give alms to the poor in accordance with your means. Receive travellers in your homes, visit the sick, show mercy to those in prison. Let women be submissive to their husbands. Let husbands never address insulting words to their wives. Let sons respect their parents and, on reaching marriageable age, take wives in lawful wedlock unless they prefer to consecrate their lives to God. Let clerics obey their Bishops, let monks faithfully observe their Rule. Let dukes, counts and other public functionaries do justice to the people and be merciful to the poor: let money not entice them from honest dealing. Nothing is hidden from God. Life is short, and the hour of death uncertain. Be always ready.[6]

We already note a modification of the old dualism between Church and State as distinct and independent societies. True, this dualism continues to exist but it is brought within the radius of a single society known as the Church or, alternatively, from the ninth century onwards, as Christendom. The Empire and monarchies on the one hand, and the priesthood on the other, are to be henceforth no more than the principal organs, the separate "ministries" of the City of God.

This conception of a *Respublica Christiana* stamped itself for several centuries on the political thought of the West. We will not maintain, as some have done, that the idea of the State temporarily vanished. The fact is rather that since the State was kept in being by the clergy, and since in that period of feudal anarchy they were the only element in society to concern themselves with the public good, the ideas of State and Church ended by becoming amalgamated in men's minds. In the twelfth century, Bishop Otto von Freising, a friend of Frederick Barbarossa, saw in this development a typical consequence of the Incarnation.

The Son of God [he wrote], coming in the flesh, chose to have Himself enrolled as a citizen of the Roman City. This City, plunged as it was in paganism, was beyond all doubt the city of this world. Why then did the Head of the City of God choose to be enrolled among its members at His birth? I can only see one possible motive: He wanted to show that

He had come down to earth so that, in a most admirable manner, He might make the City of this world into His own City.[7]

And the same prelate avowed, in his Chronicle, that the Augustinian theme of the Two Cities had almost ceased to apply, for since the days of Charlemagne, it was no longer a tale of two Cities that was being told but that of a single City, the City of God.[8]

The six-century-long absence of laymen from the field of culture and political science, the progressive establishment of a Christendom of which priesthood and empire are alike instruments, are two facts which gave to the spiritual primacy a new emphasis and significance. How could the ecclesiastical power, constantly called upon as it was by the princes to supply them with information and advice, avoid coming to regard as normal its far-reaching interventions in the temporal sphere? Were not the civil power and the ecclesiastical power both in churchmen's hands? And, in the Church, was it not the superior power which must supervise what happened and keep watch over its auxiliary with a view to rectifying its aberrations? We thus see how, by means of a simple logical process and under the pressure of events, the Church's power in the temporal sphere was increased.

Even under Louis the Pious, the feeble successor of Charlemagne, the bishops' pretensions became more marked. Indeed, they were not afraid to call their sovereign to account when he tried to arrange for a modification in the parcelling-up of the Empire which would benefit his son, Charles the Bald. They asked him to justify his stewardship—*ministerium sibi commissum*; and, having been conducted to the Church of St. Médard at Soissons, in October, 834, the unfortunate King had to make a sort of public confession and assume penitent's garb.[9]

The Papacy was to assert itself a little later with remarkable vigour. For a long time, however, the Popes were content to make use of excommunication as their sole weapon against a guilty sovereign. The great Pope Nicholas I (858-867), who threatened to anathematize Lothair II, King of Lorraine, claimed no more than the "spiritual sword".[10] But centuries

later, at the time of the famous quarrel of the Investitures,
Gregory VII went very much further. On two occasions, in
1076 and 1080, he excommunicated and deposed the King of
Germany, Henry IV, at the same time releasing his subjects
from their oath of allegiance. The kingly office, being now no
more than a "ministry" of the Church, had thus come to
depend on the Holy See for its exercise and its validity. Nothing
could be more significant in this respect than the grounds given
for the sentence of 1080: since earthly dignities were now within
the Church's province, they fell *ipso facto* under the jurisdiction
of Peter, under his divine right of binding and loosing. Addressing the Fathers of the Roman Synod, Gregory VII
exclaimed:

> Make certain now, I pray you, most holy Fathers and
> Lords, that the entire world understand and know that, if
> you can bind and loose in Heaven, you can here on earth
> remove from, and give to, each one according to his merits,
> empires, kingdoms, principalities, duchies, marquisates,
> counties, and all the possessions of men. Often you have
> deprived perverse and unworthy men of patriarchates,
> primacies, archbishoprics, bishoprics to give them to truly
> religious men. If you are then able to form judgments on
> spiritual things, what power must you not have over the
> things of this world?[11]

The oddest thing is that the guilty party himself was not in
total disagreement regarding principles with his august ad-
versary. If he claimed to hold his Crown by God's grace only,
he none the less made this all-important concession: "I cannot
be deposed for any crime unless—which God forbid—I have
erred in matters of faith."[12] In other words, on the admission
of the Emperor Henry IV, the crime of heresy was an adequate
cause for deposition; kingship having become subject to the
Church, the Sovereign lost his rights if he abandoned the Faith.

The successors of Gregory VII applied in their turn and by
different methods the principle of Papal jurisdiction over
*temporalia*. Gregory VII had claimed that this right could be
exercised in the event of grave faults or sins being committed
by a King.[13] The other Pontiffs of the medieval period went
further than this, and justified their interventions in secular

matters by the necessity of consulting—even against the Sovereign's will—the superior interests of the Church and of Christendom. At the end of the eleventh century, Pope Urban II organized the Crusade by means of direct negotiation with the great lords of the West. Their suzerains, the Kings of France and of Germany, were not even consulted. Indeed they scarcely could have been, seeing that both were at the moment excommunicated!

Under Innocent III (1198-1216) the Papacy reached the zenith of its political power. The Pontiff examined the claims of candidates to the Imperial Crown, organized the Crusade against the Albigensian heresy, deposed the King of England, John Lackland; he established round St. Peter's Throne a ring of vassal monarchies. It is from his reign that the characteristic expression "secular arm"—to signify the civil power—would seem to date. If, like Innocent III, we interpret this by the symbolism of the Anointing in the coronation ceremony (the bishop is anointed on the head and the emperor on the right arm) we see that it gives prominence to the subjection of the prince to the papal authority. The Pope is the head of Christendom, the Emperor is no more than his "arm", the agent of execution for material needs.

Another formula of this period gives in substance the same teaching: "The Pope possesses the two swords"—the spiritual sword and the temporal sword. Based on the allegorical interpretation of a scriptural text—*Ecce due gladii hic* (Luke xxii. 38)—this formula seems to date back to St. Bernard and John of Salisbury. Popes Gregory IX and Innocent IV made use of it in the ninth century in their fight against the Emperor Frederick II. It is also to be found in the celebrated Bull *Unam Sanctam* which Boniface VIII issued at the height of his conflict with Philip the Fair (1302) and we think it worth quoting the relevant context, the general tenor of which closely recalls certain of St. Bernard's expressions:

> We are instructed by the words of the Gospel that two swords are in the power of Peter, the spiritual and the temporal. In fact, when the Apostles said: "There are two swords here", i.e. in the Church, the Lord did not reply: "That is too much", but "That is enough". Certainly he

who denies that the temporal sword is in Peter's power forgets the Lord's word: "Put back thy sword in its sheath." Both swords are thus in the power of the Church, the material and the spiritual, but the former is wielded on behalf of the Church, the latter by the Church; the latter by the hand of the priest, the former by the hand of king or knight, on the word, and with the consent, of the priest. It is in fact needful that one sword should be below the other and that the temporal authority should be subject to the spiritual power.[14]

Whilst this document doubtless makes it clear that the Pope does not use the temporal sword and the spiritual sword in the same manner, it could not be more explicitly stated that both swords belong to the Church.

It is to this period, moreover, that we can trace back the theory of the "direct power" which claims to provide a genuine theological basis for the jurisdiction of the Pope over temporal affairs. This doctrine has at different times been attributed to all the great medieval Popes, beginning with Gregory VII. In fact, however, it is not correct to group together indiscriminately as advocates of this theory all those who would extend the divine right of binding and of loosing to secular affairs. It is here a question of finding out by what right— direct or indirect, normal or exceptional—the Pope can claim to possess the material (as well as the spiritual) sword. Now, in the eyes of believers in the *direct power*, the spiritual power *includes* the temporal: the one is no more than an emanation of the other. Christ who is at once Priest and King has delegated to Peter and his successors the whole of His power. The Pope possesses, in principle, all jurisdiction in civil as well as in religious affairs. In feudal language, he has a direct right of "eminent domain" over everything—and at the epoch, let us remember, "eminent domain" meant real ownership.[15] As for the use of his powers, in actual practice the Pope ordinarily exercised the spiritual power only. By Christ's own Will, he was obliged to delegate to earthly kings and princes the normal exercise of the secular power. He only took over this power in grave circumstances, by reason of sin (*ratione peccati*), during a vacancy of the Imperial throne or when it was necessary, at some critical moment, for him to take action in the higher interests of Christendom.

We have no room to sketch, in these pages, the history of a theory which allows of many different shades of emphasis. Two characteristic quotations must here suffice to indicate the essential features of the doctrine of the "direct power".

The qualities of inferior things [wrote Giacomo di Viterbo[16] in the time of Boniface VIII] are contained in superior things, effects are present in their causes. In conformity with these principles, the temporal power, which is related to the spiritual power as the inferior quality to the superior and as the effect to its cause, is comprised in the spiritual power. This is why it is taught that the rights of heavenly and earthly rule have alike been bestowed on Peter by Christ. Peter and, after him, any of his successors, in whom resides the plenitude of spiritual power, possesses for this very reason the temporal power also, not in the same manner as the secular power, but in a superior, a more exalted, manner. He does not indeed hold this power in order—except in certain cases—to carry out its functions directly; but he carries them out in a nobler manner, that is, by making use of the prince's co-operation in order to attain his own ends. Thus the temporal power pre-exists in the spiritual power in a superior degree though not, generally or normally, in the sense that it is exercised by the spiritual power.

Forty years later, at the time of the conflict between the Emperor, Ludwig of Bavaria and the Papacy, the Franciscan theologian Alvaro Pelayo wrote in similar terms:[17]

We do not, it is true, read in the Gospel that Christ gave Peter the temporal power, but we must reply that he on whom what is essential has been conferred has *ipso facto* received the accessories. Christ, in bestowing on Peter the spiritual power, which is the principal thing, undoubtedly also conferred on him the temporal power. And since this pre-exists in the spiritual power, as the inferior power pre-exists in the superior, the conclusion follows that, in bestowing the keys of the Kingdom of Heaven, Christ gave to Peter at once the temporal and the spiritual jurisdiction.

The theory of the direct power has been fairly widespread in the West since the thirteenth century and certainly influenced the ideas of Innocent IV and Boniface VIII. There are distinct inklings of it in the preamble to the Bull *Unam Sanctam*. It has never, however, been imposed in the Church as an accepted and indisputable doctrine. It is doubtless for this reason that the final definition in the above-mentioned Bull goes no further than proclaiming in general terms the universal jurisdiction of the Sovereign Pontiff.

We have thought it necessary to set out in some detail the exact circumstances in which, during the Middle Ages, the Holy See extended its jurisdiction over temporal affairs. This development was, in our opinion, justified by circumstances. During the long apprenticeship of the nations which followed on the collapse of the Roman Empire—whilst the intellect of the lay community slumbered—the Church assumed, almost unaided, the intellectual and moral leadership of civilization. How can one reproach the Papacy, in such conditions, for having become—at the zenith of the feudal period—the arbiter of the Christian world? As a matter of fact we find that recent historians are no longer content to dismiss as mere vulgar climbers men of the calibre of a Gregory VII or an Innocent III. They have attained to a fairer view of the civilizing function of the medieval Papacy and of the educative influence of the Church on the young nations of the West.

A desire to do justice to the Church does not necessarily mean however that we should attribute to all the acts of her magisterium a universally binding character. Many of them indeed had no more than a conditional value and need be accepted as only appropriate to certain stages of civilization. At other epochs the same acts might have amounted to an abuse of power. Like pedagogical methods, those of the Church need to be adapted to the age and the cultural level of her children. We cannot appeal indiscriminately to the words and deeds of the medieval Papacy as proving a right to supreme jurisdiction in political matters. Because Innocent III intervened in the Imperial elections, are we to conclude that the Holy See has the right, in order to further the Church's higher interests, to intervene directly to-day in the election of the

President of a Republic? Because Urban II organized the Crusades, without paying the faintest attention to the wishes of the King of France or the King of Germany, are we to conclude that the right of launching Crusades is inherent in the Papal jurisdiction? Because Gregory VII and several other Popes have deposed Kings, are we to see in those extreme measures the exercise of a right permanently possessed by the Holy See? And let this be clear, it is far from our intention to call in question the right of the Papacy to impose spiritual sentences, to bind the consciences of the faithful in a manner which may have repercussions in the temporal sphere. What seems to us excessive is the attempt to include in the normal jurisdiction of the Sovereign Pontiff acts of a directly temporal character which only the very special conditions of a past civilization could justify. Do not in fact let us be more exacting than Pius IX when, soon after the Vatican Council, he expressed himself clearly at an Audience on the subject of the deposition of kings:[18]

> This right has in fact—in exceptional circumstances—been exercised by the Popes; but it has nothing to do with Papal Infallibility. Its source was not the Infallibility, but the authority, of the Pope. The latter, according to the public law then in force and by the consent of the Christian nations, who recognized the Pope as the supreme Judge of Christendom, extended to judging, even in the temporal field, both Princes and States. Now the present situation is altogether different. Bad faith alone can confuse things and epochs so diverse. As though an infallible judgment in regard to a revealed Truth had any analogy with a right which the Popes, acting on the expressed desire of the nations, have exercised when the public welfare so required!

Pius IX, as we see, lays great stress on human law, custom, the consent of the nations, as forming a basis for the old Papal jurisdiction over sovereigns. We may add that, in those times, the ecclesiastical hold over the temporal power was but a reflexion of the accepted doctrine that the papacy and empire were distinct departments of a single Christian whole. In any case and as is made clear by the words of the great Pope whom we have just quoted, the practice of the Church of the Middle

3*

Ages in matters political cannot be invoked as constituting anything in the nature of an universal rule; and still less can we accept as an admissible doctrine the theory of the direct power.

The modern age was in fact to provide the Church with many opportunities for new experiments and for serious reflexion.

\*        \*        \*

From the twelfth century onwards, far-reaching developments took place in the West. Using the crumbling baronial system as a stepping-stone, young national monarchies now took their rise: in England, first, after the Norman Conquest—then in France and Spain. Contemporaneously with the rise of the kings, the laity once again made its appearance in the cultural world, especially in the realm of law. Were not lawyers needed to maintain, against the Pope if need be, the rights of the Sovereign? So it was that the teaching of Roman Law, which had been interrupted during the earlier medieval period, was resumed in Italy at the beginning of the twelfth century, and then in France under Philip Augustus. Under this influence was reborn the idea of the independent State, distinct from the Church in the same way as the old Roman Empire had once been distinct—the idea, in fact, of the State as a great secular power, not as a mere administrative unit of the ecclesiastical system. It was soon after this that the rediscovery of Aristotle's *Politics* influenced men's minds in the same direction. In its first Latin translation this treatise became known in the West in about 1260. The State, of which it explained the origin, was here presented as a natural product of human evolution, deriving from the life of the family and then from that of the village—as a "perfect society" based on natural law, without any aid from Revelation. So it was that, as from the end of the thirteenth century, Roman Law and Aristotelian philosophy combined to furnish the new national State—now well launched—with a justification for its independence *vis-à-vis* the spiritual power.

From this time forward, a complete reversal of the former situation took place. The State—particularly after the sixteenth century and following upon the Wars of Religion—gradually became secularized. Not content with claiming its independence *vis-à-vis* the Papal authority, it endeavoured, by an extension of its own sovereignty, to include the Church within its jurisdiction and to exert a rigorous control over ecclesiastical discipline. The modern State aimed at substituting the jurisdiction of the civil power over spiritual affairs for the old Papal jurisdiction over temporal affairs. It refrained indeed from interfering in the doctrinal field, but in return for this abstention showed itself all the more exacting in its supervision of the administration of the Church, her discipline and her liturgy. Thus in 1729, by one of time's revenges, the *Parlement* of Paris condemned as prejudicial to the Royal authority the new legend about Gregory VII which Pope Benedict XIII had had inserted in the Roman Breviary![19]

In face of an offensive on this scale, the Papacy—as we can easily imagine—was unable to maintain intact its medieval claims. As the modern period wore on, the Church's interventions in temporal matters became progressively rarer, and they assumed, when they did occur, a more strictly religious character. Two events marked the decline of the Papacy as a great temporal power. Of these the first was the quarrel between Boniface VIII and Philip the Fair. The outcome of this controversy, *à propos* the respective rights of King and Pope over the French clergy, was a grave humiliation for the Holy See. On the 7th September, 1303, the eve of the day on which the Bull was to appear which would have excommunicated Philip IV and released his subjects from their oath of fidelity, the armed bands of Guillaume de Nogaret stormed the palace at Anagni, insulted the Pope and held him prisoner. Freed on the following day by Cardinal Fieschi, the unfortunate Pontiff was brought back to Rome, where he died a month later. The position of the Holy See during its struggle with Ludwig of Bavaria appeared at first sight to be more favourable, for—originally excommunicated in 1324 by John XXII—the Emperor was deposed by Clement VI in 1346 and died in the following year. His successor, Charles IV, however, instead of showing favour to the Pope to whom he owed his crown, took steps, by means of the Golden Bull (1356), to put a definite stop to Papal participation in the Imperial election. The Emperor-Elect no longer awaited confirmation from Rome before assuming power.

In the modern epoch, we can still point to certain celebrated Papal acts which had to do with matters temporal. Their lack of efficacy bears witness, however, to the fact that the nations having once reached their maturity were no longer prepared to accept the overlordship, in political matters, of the spiritual power. After the discovery of America, in 1493, a Bull of Alexander VI assigned zones of influence to Spain and Portugal.[20] It is still a matter of dispute amongst historians whether the Papacy was claiming the right to divide the New World between two colonial powers, or whether it only had in view the organization of its missionary apostolate. Actually the question is only of academic interest, for as soon as a third power, namely France, established herself in America, she chose—despite the protests of Spain—to regard the pontifical decision as of no effect. Nor did any other nation pay it any further attention.

A little later, in 1570, Pius V excommunicated Queen Elizabeth on grounds of heresy and proclaimed her deposition.[21] This act was fully in conformity with medieval tradition, all the more so as the Queen was guilty of heresy; but unfortunately it did not merely prove useless, but—thanks to the conspiracies by foreign powers to which it gave rise—it considerably increased the difficulties of the English Catholics who were henceforth suspected of treason. We should not, however, feel any particular astonishment at an action which, at this distance of time, we are tempted to regard as an unfortunate anachronism. At that period the heresy of a Sovereign was still regarded, by a large section of public opinion, as invalidating his or her right to govern. Henri Quatre discovered this to his cost when he tried originally to obtain the Crown whilst remaining a Huguenot. The very thing which renders the history of the sixteenth century so tragic is the fact that the medieval conceptions of a united Christendom survived at a time when national policy was veering more and more decisively towards independent and secular aims. The Papacy, as is understandable, remained faithful to the traditional ideal and can hardly be reproached for doing so in view of the fact that the Protestant schism had not yet come to be regarded as final and irremediable.

Once this period of confusion was over, the Holy See concentrated more and more upon its spiritual mission whilst at the same time defending the clergy against the progressive encroachments of the secular monarchies. Any who suppose, however, that the Church took this line simply because she had no choice and that she remained nostalgic for her past glories show but little understanding of the adaptability of the Church's rulers or of the keen appreciation which they showed of their true mission. Confronted by the rise of the national powers, the Papacy did not remain blind or inactive. On reflexion it came to understand better that the primacy of the spiritual must gradually abandon its pretensions to despotic political authority. This external power might have had its uses when the nations were still in swaddling bands; it was but normal however that it should be toned down in this modern age in order to avoid any confusion as regards the respective missions of Church and State. Thus the modern Papacy, having definitely ceased to intervene directly in the political field, remains on its own ground, which is spiritual and moral. It no longer makes its superiority over the temporal felt by temporal means, such as the deposition of a prince, the citation before its tribunal of two political rivals, the organization of a military enterprise. No, the modern Papacy asserts itself in temporal affairs only when politics trench upon moral and spiritual matters, and then only by enlightening men's consciences and by imposing, if need be, ecclesiastical censures.

Since the seventeenth century, all Papal decisions regarding political affairs have been in conformity with this new spirit. When, in 1648, Innocent X protested in a Papal Brief against the Peace of Westphalia, he did not condemn *en bloc* all the clauses of the Treaty; he was content to declare null in conscience all those of its provisions which were prejudicial to the health of souls or to the rights of the Catholic religion.[22] At the end of the succeeding century, the Briefs of Pius VI condemning the Civil Constitution of the Clergy undoubtedly led to grave political repercussions, but the Pope did not go outside the spiritual field. Indeed, actuated by a magnanimous spirit of compassion, and in order not to have to excommunicate King Louis XVI, who had sanctioned the fatal Constitution, he actually refrained from excommunicating those who had taken the oath.[23] We again meet this spirit of forbearance in the excommunication of Napoleon by Pius VII in 1809. The Bull penalized, together with the Emperor, all who had taken part in the spoliation of the Papal States but the Pope, anxious to guard against all disorder of a temporal variety, added the following clause to the document:[24]

> We expressly forbid—under holy obedience—all Christian peoples, and particularly Our own subjects, to make use of these present letters, in order, under whatever pretext, to cause any harm to those against whom the present censure is directed—whether in respect of their goods, or of their rights and prerogatives.

In more recent times, Papal interventions closely affecting politics have been but rare. On several occasions the Holy See has condemned as null and void certain measures passed by different governments. We may instance the decrees of the Spanish Government against Religious Orders (1835); the Articles of Baden which claimed to establish, in the Swiss Catholic Cantons, a kind of Civil Constitution of the Clergy (1834); the French Law of Separation (1905). But these declarations merely brought into prominence the rôle of the Papacy, in the spiritual field, as judge of public acts and their morality. They addressed themselves only to men's consciences and were without any strictly legal effects in the temporal sphere. There has indeed been much discussion regarding the *non expedit*, whereby Pius IX, in protestation against the annexation of the Papal States, forbade Italian Catholics to take part in the parliamentary elections. This self-denying ordinance, however, attacked the Italian Government only through the consciences of individual Catholics and prescribed no positive action against the new Italy. We may add that no threat of censures was adjoined to the Pontifical document.[25]

In any case it is not by means of such prohibitions, censures and decrees of nullity that the supreme authority of the spiritual power makes itself principally felt at the present day, but rather in those admirable Encyclicals in which the Holy See recalls to the nations and to their governments the great Christian principles which should govern political, social, economic and international affairs. From Leo XIII to Pius XII in particular, the *magisterium* of the Church has affirmed with unsurpassed authority its right to express its views on all the great problems concerning human life and culture. In other days the Holy See led the still infant nations by the hand and took to task their princes. Nowadays, where adult nations are concerned, it is no longer by means of such temporal procedure that the Church asserts her pre-eminence; she does so instead by means of teachings, the magisterial character of which commands respect. The action of the Papacy on the modern world thus shows itself to be eminently spiritual in character. This does not mean that believers regard its commands as any less imperative; indeed, just as they consider themselves bound by the prohibitions of the Church, so they pride themselves on their filial obedience to the rulings of her *magisterium*.

### NOTES TO CHAPTER IV

1 Migne, *Patrol. Lat.*, LXII, pp. 68, 69.
2 Acts iv. 20; v. 19.
3 St. Augustine, *De Civitate Dei*, V, 24. *P.L.*, XLI, 171.
4 St. Gregory I, *Register*, III, 61.
5 G. Schnürer, *L'Eglise et la civilisation au Moyen Age*, Paris, 1933–38, II, p. 417.
6 Monum. Germaniae Historica, *Capitularia*, edition of Boretius, I, p. 239. Cf. H. X. Arquillière, *L'Augustinisme politique*, Paris, 1934, p. 118.
7 *Chronicon*, III, 6: Pertz, Hanover, 1867, pp. 181–182.
8 *Ibid.*, V, prol., p. 218.
9 H. X. Arquillière, *op. cit.*, p. 129.
10 Gratian, C.6, *Inter Laec*, C.XXXIII.q.2.
11 Gregory VII, *Registrum*, VII, 14, a; ed. Caspar, Berlin, 1930, p. 487.
12 Mon. Germ. Hist., *Const. et Acta.*, I, pp. 109–110.
13 *Registr.*, VIII, 21, p. 557.

[14] Lo Grasso, *Ecclesia et Status : Fontes Selecti*, Rome, 1939, pp. 188–190. Cf. J. Lecler, *L'Argument des Deux Glaives*, in the *Recherches de Science Religieuse*, 1931, pp. 299–339; 1932, pp. 151–177, 280–303.

[15] J. Lecler, *Propriété et Féodalité* in *Etudes*, 20 May, 1934, pp. 433–449.

[16] G. di Viterbo, *De Regimine Christiane*, II, 7; edited by H. X. Arquillière, under the name *Le plus ancien Traité de l'Eglise*, Paris, 1926, pp. 236–237. At the same period, Giles of Rome wrote, for his part: "Materialis gladius suam potestatem habet a Summo Pontifice, cum omnis potestas quae est in ecclesia militante est a Summo Pontifice derivata" (*De Ecclesiastica Potestate*, III, 3; published by Scholz, Weimar, 1929, p. 158)

[17] *De Planctu Ecclesiae*, I, 57; Roccaberti, *Bibliotheca Pontificia*, III, pp. 172–173.

[18] *Civilta Cattolica*, VIII Series, Vol. 3, 1871, p. 485. These words were pronounced on the 20th July, 1871, to a delegation of the Accademia di Religione Cattolica.

[19] G. Hardy, *Le Cardinal de Fleury et le mouvement janséniste*, Paris, 1925, p. 166.

[20] Lo Grasso, *Ecclesia et Status*, pp. 199–203. Cf. J. Lecler, *Autour de la Donation d'Alexandre VI* in *Etudes*, 5 and 20 October, 1938.

[21] Lo Grasso, *op. cit.*, pp. 209–211.

[22] *Bullarium Romanum*, Turin, 1867, Vol. XV, p. 603.

[23] Letter from Cardinal Zelada to Mgr. Salamon, quoted by J. Gendry, *Pie VI*, Paris, 1906, p. 149.

[24] Cardinal Pacca, *Mémoires pour servir à l'Histoire ecclésiastique du XIXe siècle*, Louvain, 1833, I, p. 111.

[25] The *non-expedit*, issued in 1874, was not abrogated until 1919. A declaration of the Holy Office, dated the 30th June 1886, had interpreted it as involving a strict prohibition: *non expedit prohibitionem importat*. Regarding its history, cf. G. Mollat, *La Question Romaine de Pie VI à Pie XI*, Paris, 1932, pp. 368 *et seq.*

# V

# THE PRIMACY OF THE SPIRITUAL: THEORIES OF INDIRECT POWER

IN studying the question of the powers to which the modern
Church lays claim in matters temporal we have so far
refrained from invoking any particular system or theory,
thinking it best to give pride of place to the attitude in fact
adopted by ecclesiastical authority. As may well be imagined,
however, theological speculation has not been at a standstill
since the rise of the national States added a further complication
to the problem of the two powers and their hierarchical
relationship. A succinct and critical study of the course taken
by these speculations will enable us to place in a clearer light
the elements which might conduce to a solution of the problem.

The theory of the "direct power" claimed to reduce to a
single origin the dual jurisdiction of State and Church.
According to this theory, the prince's power was a kind of
delegated authority, an emanation of the Papal *magisterium*.
Sprung from a background of medieval culture, this theory
was destined to vanish together with the epoch which gave it
birth. Still much in evidence at the end of the sixteenth
century—St. Robert Bellarmine was familiar with it—the
whole idea has now so completely disappeared from sight
that many moderns have little notion of the important part
which it played in the theological world of those days.

The same cannot be said of the rival theory which was
introduced at the outset of the modern age: the theory known
as that of the "indirect power". This has never been
"canonized" by the Holy See but it can claim authoritative
backing from that quarter. Pius IX in fact condemned in his

*Syllabus* the following proposition, extracted from Nuytz's "Treatise on Ecclesiastical Law": "The Church has no temporal power, either direct or indirect."[1] In 1913, on the occasion of the 37th Congress of Catholic Lawyers, Cardinal Merry del Val, the Papal Secretary of State, wrote to Cardinal Sevin, Archbishop of Lyons, to put the participants in the Congress on their guard against certain errors in political matters. Catholic writers, he remarked, are not always free from such errors, "particularly when they think of the two societies—civil and ecclesiastical—as simply *co-ordinated* with each other, or when they reduce to a merely *directive* authority the *indirect jurisdiction* which the Church has the right to exert over temporal affairs when these have a supernatural aspect."[2]

\*     \*     \*

If we trace the theory of the indirect power to its source, we shall see that it well fitted the new situation resulting from the appearance in the Christian world of the national States. This theory fully recognizes, as facts which have to be taken into account, that the State can no longer be considered as a mere administrative department of the Church and that the political society, which differs in origin and aim from the spiritual society, has an independent existence of its own.

Basing itself upon Aristotle's *Politics*, on which he had written a commentary, St. Thomas Aquinas pointed out that, because of its purely human and natural origin, the government of pagan kings remained, even after the advent of Christ, perfectly lawful:

> Infidelity is not in itself incompatible with political power, since the latter owes its origin to the law of nations which is a human law; the distinction between the faithful and infidels, which arises from Divine law, does not automatically cancel human law.[3]

Corresponding to the human origin of the State is its principal end which is the material welfare of man, the Church being concerned with his spiritual welfare:

> As it was the function of secular princes to issue positive decrees based on Natural Law, with a view to the common temporal good, so it was the function of the rulers of the

Church to frame spiritual laws for the general welfare of the faithful.[4]

Thus, for St. Thomas and his school, the State was a "perfect society", a sovereign power like the Church. A practical conclusion from this view was that the young national States were within their rights in pursuing an independent policy in accordance with the genius of their respective peoples. The Angelic Doctor was, however, careful to point out that their independence in respect of the Church could not be absolute. For the earthly aims of the political society were necessarily subordinate to matters pertaining to eternal salvation, the supreme purpose of the spiritual society. When man's salvation is at stake, the State must yield to the Church and obey her:

> The spiritual power and the secular power both derive their origin from the Divine Power. This means that the secular power is subordinate to the spiritual power in the measure decreed by God, that is to say, in all matters concerning the salvation of souls; for in such things it is more profitable to obey the spiritual rather than the secular power.[5]
> The secular power is subject to the spiritual as the body is subject to the soul. It is for this reason that there is no usurpation when the spiritual superior intervenes regarding those particular temporal matters in which the secular power is subject to him . . . [6]

St. Thomas had no occasion to develop any further these political considerations. Nevertheless, by affirming the sovereignty of the State in its own order, together with its partial subordination to the Church in all that is concerned with salvation, he laid the foundations of the doctrine of the Indirect Power.

At this point, however, a problem presents itself which is worth investigating. We are in fact faced with the question whether the theory of the Indirect Power, as set forth by Cardinal Bellarmine, is the only one which can claim to be in accordance with the above principles and, consequently, with the ideas of St. Thomas.

We may at once set aside the theory of Dante, according to

which the Pope is in duty bound to give enlightenment and advice to the Emperor, whilst the Emperor is obliged to show the Pope the reverence due from an eldest son to his father;[7] for here we have no more than a *directive* power, as Fénelon calls it,[8] i.e. that of a simple spiritual father whose authority is not exercised by command but merely by suasion.

Quite a different attitude was adopted by a disciple of St. Thomas, the Dominican John of Paris, whose treatise *De potestate regia et papali*[9] was written in about 1303 when the struggle between Rome and Philip the Fair was at its height. This work, which is inspired by Thomist principles regarding the natural right of the State, surpasses them in precision. The author, like his master, teaches that the political society is subordinate to the spiritual society but explains in his own original and persuasive manner what this in fact involves in the event of a grave conflict. Ecclesiastical jurisdiction, he writes, is only spiritual, and cannot directly inflict any but spiritual penalties (*non est nisi spiritualis directe*). It has certainly the right to intervene in temporal matters in the event of a moral fault to which they have given rise or of which they are the occasion (*ratione peccati*). Even in this case, however, the Church's coercive power would not enable her, except in an indirect and incidental manner (*indirecte et per accidens*) to do more than inflict spiritual censures. An example will suffice to demonstrate how this indirect action of the spiritual power is in the nature merely of a repercussion or after-effect. Supposing we have a heretical King, incorrigible and contemptuous of ecclesiastical penalties. The Pope cannot, in any circumstances, himself proclaim his deposition; but, once he has launched a decree of excommunication against this King, it becomes a meritorious act on the part of the Christian subjects to whom he has caused scandal to deprive him of his crown and remove him from the throne. Thus the Papal action will have indirectly brought about the sovereign's deposition. It can be said in the same way, John of Paris writes elsewhere, that the *magisterium* of the Church, exerting authority over men's consciences, acts indirectly on *temporalia* (*indirecte possunt in temporalibus*) by causing a sense of justice and of charity to permeate little by little the social life of mankind.

The theory of Cardinal Bellarmine, although derived from the same formulae, is very far from making the same impression, and really amounts to no more than the revival of a scholastic tradition dating back to the beginning of the fourteenth century. The illustrious author of the "Controversies" (1576-1588) gives much prominence to the purely spiritual character of the Papal authority. Before him, certain theologians, such as the Dominican Francesco di Vittoria, had expressed approval of the following formula: "When he has a spiritual aim in view, the Pope possesses a real temporal authority over kings and emperors."[10] Bellarmine rightly rejects this maxim which is too theocratic in tendency and which might give rise to erroneous ideas in regard to the true nature of ecclesiastical jurisdiction. His pertinent comments on the respective characters of the two powers did not however prevent Bellarmine from pushing much further than John of Paris the extent to which the Papal authority might be held to possess a hold over temporal affairs. The indirect power which he attributed to the Church was something more than the temporal repercussion of a purely spiritual action:

We understand by indirect jurisdiction that which the Sovereign Pontiff possesses over temporal things in view of a spiritual end. The Papal power is specifically and of its very nature spiritual in character and it only aims directly, and as the first object of its activity, at spiritual affairs. Indirectly, however, that is to say when such means are necessary in order to obtain spiritual ends, it intervenes also in temporal affairs, which are regarded as a secondary object with which the spiritual power is only concerned in exceptional circumstances.[11]

According to this theory, the expression "indirect power" is used simply as a synonym for *exceptional* power. It is only exercised when grave spiritual interests are found to be at stake; but on such occasions it intervenes directly without making use of any kind of intermediary. In the eyes of John of Paris, the Pope is regarded as having indirect power over the Prince because a spiritual censure pronounced against the latter may have the effect of inciting his people to depose him:

the temporal results are in the nature of an after-effect. Bellarmine's view, on the other hand, is that the Pope has indirect power over the Prince because in the case of the latter's committing a serious crime or falling into heresy, the Papal sentence can decree not only his excommunication but his deposition as well; temporal consequences are thus attained directly, even though the intervention which leads to them be exceptional in character. We have chosen this extreme case, because it is one that is familiar to the two authors quoted. It serves to illustrate the difference which, despite their common basis and analogous phrasing, divides the two theories.

\*　　\*　　\*

What are we to think of these theories? and how can they be harmonized with the experience of the Church, as we have endeavoured to describe it? The Bellarmine theory can claim the support of numerous eminent authorities. Quite recently, M. Journet, following upon M. Maritain, has learnedly defended it in his book: *La Jurisdiction de l'Eglise sur le Cité* (Paris, 1931). Our own considered view however is that the theory suffers from being unduly bound up with the outworn trammels of medieval civilization. In this connexion we may note a curious and significant detail. After having carefully proved the existence of the two sovereignties, that of the Church and that of the State, Bellarmine subsequently claims to amalgamate them in a single organism of which the Pope is head:

> However, when princes are Christian and are numbered amongst the members and sons of the Church, the two Powers are so closely linked together that they form but a single *respublica*, a single kingdom, a single family, even a single body. We are indeed, according to the Apostle, one single body in Christ, and we are, all and singular, members of one another. But in this mystical body of the Church, the ecclesiastical power represents the mind, the political power the body.[12]

We thus come back, after a digression, to the old medieval idea of a unique society with its two sets of ministers, spiritual and temporal. After this it will not surprise us if the Bellarmine theory, although starting from such different premisses, reaches in practice the same conclusions as the rival theory of the direct power. The new theory, just like the old, permits the Pope to intervene directly in secular affairs and even to depose the Prince in virtue of a kind of *raison d'Eglise* which has some analogy with the *raison d'Etat*.[13] There is here, as a little reflexion plainly shows, a certain lack of coherence. Why insist against Vittoria and others on the uniquely spiritual character of the Papal jurisdiction if in fact the Pope is entitled, in exceptional cases, to act like an earthly sovereign? Based on very solid premisses, the Bellarmine theory never arrives at the conclusions towards which, at the beginning, it seemed to tend. It is not surprising that, up to our own time, it has often met either with reserves or with opposition. St. Francis of Sales himself, without showing any desire to examine the theory in detail, displayed anxiety regarding the threat to which it seemed to expose rulers. He wrote in 1611 to Bénigne Milletot:[14]

No, I have not found to my taste certain writings by a holy and most excellent Prelate in which he has touched upon the indirect power of the Pope over princes: not that I have formed my judgment as to whether things are, or are not, as he says, but because, in this age, in which we have so many external enemies, I do not think that we ought to cause any commotion inside the body of the Church. The poor mother hen who shelters us, her chickens, under her wings, has enough difficulty in defending us from the hawk without its being necessary for us to peck at each other and agitate her. Again, if kings and princes are going to have a bad impression of their spiritual father, as of one whose wish is to catch them unawares and to mulct them of the authority in which God, the Sovereign Father, Prince and King of all, has given them a share, what will be the effect other than to alienate their affections to a dangerous extent? And if they believe that he is being false to his duty, will they not be tempted to be false to theirs?

We may remind ourselves also that Pius IX, whose words we have already quoted, was not only far from regarding the deposition of kings as a right of "eminent" spiritual power, but saw in it no more than a transitory prerogative bound up with the civilization of the Middle Ages and with the customs and public law of that epoch.

Must we therefore reject Bellarmine's version of the theory of the Indirect Power? Certainly not its principles which are unassailable. It would seem, however, to be incumbent on the modern theologian to maintain to the full the logic of this first affirmation: the power of the Church is purely spiritual. Embarrassed by contemporary events—for the deposition of Elizabeth by Pius V dates from 1570—it looks as though Bellarmine had been driven to a compromise. The attitude of the Papacy in these last centuries, the Encyclicals of Leo XIII and of Pius XI, would seem however to authorize us to carry the argument to a more logical conclusion. As we have already emphasized, the kaleidoscope of changing relationships between the two powers never in practice permits the Church to have exclusive recourse to solutions which proved acceptable in the past.

*         *         *

All things considered, the solution suggested by John of Paris seems more in conformity than does Bellarmine's with the true nature of the Church and with her mission in this world. This solution undoubtedly owes much to French tradition and to its two leading characteristics: deep attachment to the Holy See, and constant concern for the independence of the monarchy where its essential prerogatives are concerned. In this solution the Pope's right to concern himself with political affairs, *ratione peccati*, is not denied; but the view taken is that the exercise of this right does not include any act that is, strictly speaking, temporal, and that excommunication is its most drastic weapon. Although this theory has always found valuable support in France we shall be careful not to call it "Gallican". In fact, there would seem to be nothing to prevent us from classifying this doctrine amongst the theories of the "Indirect Power". Not only is it based, like Bellarmine's theory, on Thomist principles, but it makes better use of the same technical phraseology. John of Paris brings out extremely well the "indirect" character of the Papal authority which only affects matters temporal through the repercussion on the material sphere of measures that are in themselves spiritual. It is not easy, on the other hand, to see how one can describe as indirect a power which, when it is exercised, affects its object directly.

During the Council of the Vatican, the French Government felt some anxiety in regard to the doctrines contained in the project *de Ecclesia*, its fear being that there might be a revival of the ancient theories on the power of the Holy See. A reply by Cardinal Antonelli, the Papal Secretary of State, dated 19th March, 1870, had the effect of calming these anxieties.[15] Indeed it made use of terminology concerning the indirect power which reflected the views of John of Paris:

> The Church has received from God the sublime mission of leading men, whether regarded individually or as a society, towards a supernatural end; she possesses then, for this very reason, the power and the duty to judge of the morality and the justice of all acts, whether internal or external, in the light both of Natural and of Divine Law.
>
> Now, since no action, whether it be ordered by a supreme power or whether it emanate from individual freewill, can be unrelated to the norms of morality and justice, it follows that the judgment of the Church, whilst it applies directly to the morality of acts, is extended indirectly to everything which has a moral aspect. This does not, however, mean that the Church intervenes directly in political affairs which, according to the order established by God and according to the teachings of the Church herself, belong to the sphere of the temporal power, independently of any other authority.

From the above we can see that, in the eyes of the Secretary of State to Pius IX, the judgments and decisions of the Church do not impinge upon the political and social world except by concomitance and through their after-effects. The phrase "indirect power" is not only well calculated to give prominence to the purely religious character of the Papal power, it also admirably brings out the nature of the action exercised by the Papacy on the world in modern times. As we have seen, the Popes of to-day no longer enter the political arena in order to play some active part there, or to overthrow established powers.

No, they address themselves, in the fullness of their authority, to men's consciences; they condemn as null and void, so far as the moral law is concerned, certain decrees and treaties drawn up by governments; they excommunicate those public authorities who violate the rights of God and the Church; above all, they enlighten and direct men's minds, recalling to individuals and to governments the principles of the Catholic religion in relation to all the leading problems of the day.

This action is universal, since all the works of man possess, for those who have eyes, a moral and spiritual aspect. As Leo XIII wrote, "everything which in human affairs is sacred for one reason or another, everything which concerns the salvation of souls and Divine worship, either in virtue of its own nature or because it is considered holy through its relationship with the spiritual: all such things come under the authority of the Church."[16] This action by the Church is juridic in character for it does not consist solely in giving enlightenment and advice; indeed, when necessary, the Church commands or forbids under the sanction of canonical censures. Yet her action remains spiritual, she only employs spiritual weapons, and abstains from herself forming parties or political organizations; only spiritual verdicts are pronounced, nor is there any intention of achieving, through these, direct effects upon the civil community. There is of course no doubt that temporal affairs will be definitely affected by the actions of the religious authority, but such effects, whether social or political, will only be, as it were, the echo or reverberation, in human society, of activity whose first objective is the conscience of man.

And how discreet and tactful the Church of to-day shows herself when taking action! One could imagine a Church which, without precisely stepping outside her own zone of influence, would yet impose upon men's consciences an intolerable load. Such a nightmare clericalism would have as disastrous effect as would the control by the Church of all public institutions. Happily no danger of this kind exists. It is true that, when the need arises, the Holy See does not hesitate to assert its authority, even by means of censures and condemnations. But, outside such extreme cases, we must recognize that the spiritual power is anxious to ensure the maximum of independence to the temporal power in everything that is not contrary to morals and to the rights of individuals and of the Church. This same solicitude for just liberty is to be noted in the directions given to Catholics in regard to political, social and economic matters. These directions, though precise, are broadminded and elastic, leaving—in the matter of application—a wide margin to consciences. On numerous occasions, narrow-minded individuals have endeavoured to obtain exclusive approbation from the ecclesiastical authority for their own pet schemes, political or social, on the grounds that these alone are in conformity with the mind of the Church. These schemes have however always been foiled, so anxious is the Holy See not to lay on men's consciences a load heavier than is required in their spiritual interests.

\*       \*       \*

Must the primacy of the spiritual be practically expressed through the rule of the City by the Church? In seeking to solve this delicate question we are faced, as the preceding pages have indicated, by the fact of an undeniable change in the attitude of the Church and her earthly Head. To those who refuse to see in the Church anything except a power of this world, a mere political organization, the conclusion seems obvious that the whole conduct of the Church in her relations with the secular powers is governed by opportunism. Like all human sovereignties, they say, she is actuated, deep down, by one aim only: that of absolute and universal domination. She is, however, a past mistress at concealing her reverses by means of changes of front and prudent withdrawals: a fact which will not prevent her, when a favourable opportunity again presents itself, from reverting, with undiminished zest, to her ancient dreams of greatness.

This naïve conclusion will prove acceptable only to those whose minds are impervious to spiritual ideas or who are completely blinded by political prejudice. In reality the Church has never forgotten either her supernatural origin or the supra-terrestrial character of her vocation. "My

Kingdom is not of this world," Christ said to Pilate, and the Church, being His Kingdom, has its centre of gravity outside this world and remote from mere earthly values. None the less, it is an essential part of the Church's destiny to dwell here below, in order to be the "light of the world" and the "salt of the earth" and in order to infuse the supernatural life into humankind. Whilst not being "of this world", the Church has nevertheless been sent "into this world,"[17] not to seclude herself from the world, but to act upon the world in a heavenly manner. It is this peculiar situation of the Church in the world—at once transcendent and immanent—that raises the all-important problem of her impact on the world, its manner and its methods. This being so, is there any reason for surprise if, at different epochs and under different civilizations, the action of the Church varies? Again, it is only through experience that the Church can learn how far, without imperilling her interior life, she can afford to make her presence felt in the secular sphere.

In the Middle Ages, the Church appears to have been greatly concerned with the external Christianization of the world: with communities and institutions, with professions and public life, with the arts and sciences. The explanation of this is to be found, as we have seen, in the social and political state of Europe after the collapse of the Roman Empire. In consequence of a long-enduring eclipse of profane thought and knowledge, the Church found herself for several centuries in the position of sole guide and directress of Western civilization. Thus it was that the primacy of the spiritual power evolved in the form of a true jurisdiction, a right of direct intervention in political affairs, which even included the power to depose kings and emperors. Such a tremendous access of external prestige was not, as events were to show, without its drawbacks. Some of these strike the historian at once: the increasing entanglement of the Church in temporal affairs, the anticlerical reactions, alike of individuals and of communities, the struggles for supremacy with the civil authorities. Other disadvantages were less apparent, but would later on show themselves to be of equal gravity. We gladly recognize that the Middle Ages gave the world an outward semblance of Christianity: but what, on the other hand, did they do to ensure that the people were truly Christian at heart, and that the clergy received the spiritual formation which they required? Such investigations as have been made into the state of religious instruction amongst the people, the education of the clergy and the intensity of sacramental life suggest that a disappointing reply must be given to this question and that little was in fact done.

When these facts are taken into consideration, the Church's change of front in the modern epoch no longer bears the likeness of a mere strategical withdrawal, but is seen rather to be the effect of a decision based on past experience, and rich in possibilities for the future. Confronted by what are now adult nations, the Church has understood more clearly the need to avoid giving any occasion for misunderstanding in regard to her own power and authority. The intense activity of Catholic Action in all grades of society; the effort that is being made at present to develop an interior life of the spirit amongst all classes of the community; the extreme reserve of the hierarchy in regard to politics and all temporal enterprises: these facts show us very clearly the direction in which the contemporary Church is setting her course. The Church of to-day still desires of course, as she always must desire, the conversion of the world; but she desires to bring it about by different methods, in a different manner. Whilst not despising surface contacts, she prefers to them those contacts which are likely to produce deep and lasting effects. Without neglecting her external prestige and the defence of her essential rights, she prefers to make an impression rather by the holiness of her members and the authoritativeness of her teaching. Although continuing to take an interest in secular institutions, she prefers to act upon human society through the agency of faithful Catholics leading a full Christian life. Against this background the primacy of the spiritual can no longer be conceived, like in the Middle Ages, as being equivalent to an external and direct domination over secular affairs. This primacy no doubt involves the right to rule, but it is a rule over souls, an authority which directs them and enlightens them in regard to the Christian principles of political and social life—the Church's rights can even be thought of as including a power over temporal things, but it is in this case an oblique and indirect power, a power which only affects earthly States and institutions in virtue of the sway which she still holds over the hearts of men and of the after-effects which spring therefrom.

## NOTES TO CHAPTER V

[1] Denzinger, *Enchiridion*, No. 1724.

[2] *Acta Apostolicae Sedis*, 1913, p. 559. The italics are to be found in the original text.

[3] 2. 2, q. 12, a. 2c.

[4] 2. 2, q. 147, a. 3c.

[5] In *II Sent.*, dist. 44, q. 2, a. 3, ad 4.

[6] 2. 2, q. 60, a. 6, ad 3.

[7] *De Monarchia*, III, 16; cf. E. Gilson, *Dante et la Philosophie*, Paris, 1939, pp. 80 *et seq.*

[8] *De Summi Pontificis auctoritate*, c. 27–28. See Fénelon, *Œuvres*, Paris, 1848, II, pp. 31 *et seq.*

[9] Edited by Dom Jean Leclercq, *Jean de Paris et l'Ecclésiologie du XIIIe siècle*, Paris, 1942. We have here made use particularly of C.XIII, pp. 211–216.

[10] *De potestate ecclesiastica*, c. 12, in his *Reflectiones theologicae*, Madrid edition, 1934, p. 76.

[11] *De potestate papae in rebus temporalibus*, c. 5; *Opera Omnia*, Naples edition, 1872, V, p. 278.

[12] *De translatione Imperii romani*, c. 12; *Opera Omnia*, V, p. 80.

[13] H. de Lubac, *Le pouvoir de l'Eglise en matière temporelle* in the *Revue des Sciences Religieuses*, 1932, p. 340. We are in agreement as regards essentials with the author of this excellent article, but we think ourselves justified in retaining for good reasons the expression "indirect power".

[14] *Œuvres*, Annecy edition, XV, pp. 95–96.

[15] *Collectio Lacensis. Acta conciliorum recentiorum*, Freiburg-im-Breisgau, 1890, VII, 1556–1557.

[16] Encyclical *Immortale Dei*.

[17] John xvii. 16, 18.

*Part Two*

Various Theories and Historical
Situations : Caesaro-Papism—
Clericalism—The Lay State

# VI

# CAESARO-PAPISM

WE have now given, in broad outline, the traditional doctrine on relations between Church and State. We are therefore in a position to examine, in the light of this doctrine, certain historical situations into which the questions of harmony between the two powers and of their respective autonomy enter, at least to some extent. This examination is not only of interest as concerning the past; it also serves to emphasize certain dangers which are still with us, certain doctrines which are more to be dreaded than ever. Our enquiries should then be of practical value and should enable us to appreciate even more highly, by force of contrast, the admirable way in which the Catholic position strikes the balance between two extremes.

Three successive theories have, in the course of the centuries, had the effect of raising further discussion on the subjects of dualism and sovereignty: these are the theories of Caesaro-papism, of Clericalism and of the Lay State. Caesaro-papism appeared in the world as a survival from the ancient State and its religious prerogatives; it tended to make the prince into Head of the Church and arbiter of religion. Clericalism is, as it were, the Church's repartee to Caesaro-papism; of medieval origin, it reflects a frequent tendency on the part of the clergy to treat the State as a servant of the Church which is bound to carry out its will. The lay State is a complex phenomenon peculiar to the modern world; it can assume the most diverse forms, ranging from the despotic control of the Church and of clerical discipline to the most liberal application of a separatist policy. These three theories and the situations to which they have given rise in history have acquired so great an importance

4

in the political world of to-day, as in that of yesterday, that we think it worth while to study them carefully.

*     *     *

Caesaro-papism is rooted in the tradition common to the whole ancient world; the prince is at the head of the religious, as he is of the civil, order of things. In Christian circles, however, it would have been impossible for him to rest his claims purely on this pagan tradition the memory of which would have inspired nothing but aversion in the minds of the faithful. It was even thought necessary by Gratian, as late as the end of the fourth century, to make sure of guarding against any survival of Caesar-worship by suppressing the Imperial title of *Pontifex Maximus*. But another tradition existed which both commanded the greatest respect and was exempt from any trace of paganism: that of the Jewish nation and the Books of the Old Testament. Here notable precedents recalled to the Christian Emperors and to their vassals that, under the Old Law, the Kings of Israel had exercised legal authority over both religious and civil affairs. David and Solomon were not even satisfied with legislating in religious matters and with treating the priests as state officials, they themselves offered sacrifices and blessed the people.[1] Another King, Josias, after the discovery of the Book of Deuteronomy in 621, had in person directed the great reform in worship as the Law commanded.[2] Later, it is true, a reaction took place in favour of the priests, as we are reminded by the history of King Ozias who was punished by leprosy because he himself burned incense in the Temple;[3] in practice, however, this amounted to no more than the reservation to priests of ritual functions, there was no question of freeing them from their allegiance to the temporal authority. These were the real precedents which were followed by the Christian Caesars and to which Kings and Emperors have not ceased to appeal, even down to our own day. Bishops and Popes might invoke, as indeed they often did, the duality of the rule established by Christ, but it was in vain that they declared—following St. Gelasius—that since the coming of Christ, the only true Priest-King, no man had the right to claim both kingship and priesthood for himself. But, whatever the Church might say, the Old Testament examples continued to exert an irresistible fascination over the princes.

Without entering into any detail regarding the history of Caesaro-papism, we would recall that, ever since ancient times, it has always been a temptation to Christian sovereigns and to the theorists who magnified their authority to fall back on this doctrine. It was not long after the conversion of the Roman Empire that this temptation at first presented itself. Mgr. Battifol and, more recently, M. Palanque, have done their best to acquit the Emperor Constantine of the charge of Caesaro-papism.[4] We should rejoice at his acquittal, but can hardly help perceiving in the Emperor's policy certain tendencies of the kind attributed to him. "The external Bishop", as he liked to be called, was very fond of intervening in ecclesiastical affairs. He convoked councils and threatened recalcitrant bishops. He enjoined St. Athanasius, under pain of deposition, to receive into the Church a group of repentant Arians. His pretensions were mild, however, compared with those of his son Constantius. At the height of the doctrinal conflicts arising out of Arianism, the latter boldly took upon himself the task of restoring spiritual unity, but in a manner which could only be to the advantage of the heretics! At the Council of Milan (355) he intervened in person, in order to force the bishops present to sign the condemnation of St. Athanasius, the champion of Nicaean orthodoxy. "Whatever I will is canonically binding," he announced to protesters, "the Syrian bishops do not make difficulties of this sort when I address *them*. The choice is obedience or exile!"[5] In order to make certain of his victory, he brought pressure to bear on Pope Liberius to pronounce the same condemnation and, when the Pontiff refused, he was removed from Rome, summoned to appear before the Emperor, and finally exiled.

The successors of Constantius did not show the same rash inclination to embrace heterodox opinions. It must indeed be admitted that the majority showed themselves genuinely zealous to defend the Church. None the less, it seemed to them right and proper to intervene frequently in purely ecclesiastical affairs. Not only that, but from about 450 onwards, they were no longer content with merely convoking councils; in fact, their enthusiasm about dogma, combined with their anxiety to find rapid solutions for theological problems, led them to introduce a remarkable innovation, according to which the Imperial Chancellery drew up a formula of faith, the acceptance of which by all might be expected to put an end to controversy; this document was then sent to the bishops with the request that they should sign, and refusal to do so was liable to mean exile or deposition. Examples of this procedure were: the Encyclical of Basiliscus (475), the Henotic of Zeno (482), the Edict of Justinian against the Three Chapters (553), the *Ecthesis* of Heraclius (634), the *Typus* of Constantine II (648). By this means the Emperors succeeded in exercising a sort of *magisterium* over the Church.

By no one was this spiritual Caesarism pushed to greater lengths than by the Emperor Justinian. Anyone who requires proof of this should read his Epistle No. VI addressed to Epiphanus, Patriarch of Constantinople.[6] It begins in apparently reassuring fashion by drawing a distinction between the two powers: "The greatest gifts that God has made to men are the priesthood and the empire, the priesthood for the ordering of divine things, the empire for that of human things." But a subsequent passage is disquieting: "The Emperors attach no greater importance to anything than they do to the respectability of the clergy and to the truth of the dogmas taught. All will be well if those holy Canons are observed which we hold from the Apostles and which the holy Fathers have preserved and explained." A list of ordinances follows concerning the choice of bishops and their consecration, the obligation of residence, the rules for admission into the clerical body and into the order of deaconesses. All the patriarchs, metropolitans, bishops and clerics are bidden to obey these prescriptions, and spiritual penalties such as excommunication are provided against delinquents. One is even forced to conclude that the Emperor imagined himself to have the right to watch over the orthodoxy of Christian teaching and to impose upon the Church dogmatic formulae of his own choice.[7]

The example set by Justinian was perpetuated for many centuries in Byzantine tradition. His successors continued to exercise over the Oriental Churches a highly despotic authority. Their interferences in doctrinal matters became rarer, it is true, after the iconoclastic controversy had been settled, but their hold on ecclesiastical administration and discipline was not relaxed. So it was that, at the beginning of the tenth century, the Emperor Leo VI, reviving the legislation of Justinian, incorporated in the new code, entitled *Basilicae*, a whole series of decrees of an ecclesiastical character. In the modern epoch, the Czar of Russia, Peter the Great, was to base the right which he claimed to reform the Church on Jewish and Byzantine tradition. The famous "Church Ordinance" which assured his spiritual power and brought into being the Holy Synod thus served to prolong, on Russian soil, the religious despotism of the Emperors of the East.[8]

The attitude of the Eastern Churches towards Caesaro-papism is hard for Western theologians to understand. We must not indeed forget that illustrious champions of the Church and of its privileges sprang from the ranks of these bodies. It is enough to recall, in this connexion, the names of St. Athanasius, of St. Maximus the Confessor, of St. John Damascene and of St. Theodore Studites. It is, however, impossible not to see at work a progressive subservience on the part of the Byzantine clergy towards the Imperial authority, nor can one help noting—a still more serious matter—the gradual adaptation of men's intellects to this slave-mentality. In the Middle Ages the acceptance of Caesaro-papism amongst Oriental canonists and theologians had become common. Theodore Balsamon (twelfth century) placed the Emperor above the Patriarch and gave, as his reason for doing so, the view that, whilst the latter only had to do with men's souls, the former was concerned with their souls and bodies. Demetrios Chromatenos (thirteenth century) made of the Emperor the common Head of the Churches and attributed to him all spiritual power save that of conferring Orders. Macarius of Ancyna (fifteenth century) finally went so far as to say: "God has entrusted to the Emperor not only the helmsmanship of the Empire, but that of the Church as well."[9]

What in fact occurred was that the Byzantine Church of the Middle Ages threw off the spiritual yoke of the Papacy, merely in order to submit unresistingly to the sway of a temporal sovereignty. Thus, with a strange levity, the Eastern Church exchanged the yoke of obedience to Rome, which distance rendered light, in order to accept the rule of an Imperial Government rendered formidable by its proximity. It is hard indeed to fathom the folly of those who restored with their own hands to the temporal authority that totalitarian power from which Christ had come to set them free.

In the West, on the other hand, the tradition of Caesaro-papism always met with powerful opposition. So far back as the reign of Constantius—in the middle of the fourth century— the most effective allies of St. Athanasius in his fight against Imperial despotism were his colleagues of Gaul, Spain and Italy. At the Council of Milan (356) Athanasius himself informs us that they warned the Emperor in strong terms "not to bring confusion into religious affairs, not to introduce the civil power into the constitution of the Church." Hosius of Cordova, Hilary of Poitiers and Lucifer de Cagliari carried on the good fight for the independence of the bishops in the spiritual field. Thirty years later, St. Ambrose, Bishop of Milan, renewed the struggle and expressed in lapidary phrases the liberty of the Church: "Divine things are not within the competence of the Imperial power; the Emperor is concerned with palaces, the Bishop with churches. . . . The Emperor is *in* the Church, he is not *above* the Church."[10] The Papacy does not seem to have intervened till later, when it did so with charac- teristic vigour. The declarations of St. Gelasius and Symmachus, which have already been quoted, were often called to mind in the ensuing controversies between the powers. We may here recall an apt reply by Gregory II to the Emperor Leo the Isaurian during the iconoclastic controversy. That crowned theologian was in the habit of calling himself Emperor and priest and of pronouncing on dogmatic questions in the most brazen manner. The Pope addressed him thus:[11]

Listen to my humble advice, O Emperor! Leave these things alone and follow the Holy Church, such as thou findest her, and believe her teachings. Dogmas are not the Emperor's affair, but that of the Bishops, because it is we who have the Spirit of Christ. Just as the Bishop has no right

to meddle in the affairs of the Palace and to distribute places
at court, so the Emperor has no right to interfere in the
affairs of the Church . . . Let each one be content with the
station to which God has called him.

In any case, from the end of the fifth century, the western
parts of the Empire were destined to escape for good from the
sway of the Caesars. With the disappearance of the Western
Emperor (476), a new era opened for this part of Christendom.
It was to be marked—as we have seen—by the growing preponderance of the Church, the custodian and originator of our
civilization. Caesaro-papism, instead of gaining ground as it
was doing in Byzantium, tended to give way more and more
to the prestige of the spiritual society.

And yet the traditions of Caesaro-papism were far from
being forgotten. They revived from time to time when a
powerful and domineering personality held sway. Moreover,
they were preserved and even developed in the works of
theorists and controversial writers.

We have already spoken of Charlemagne and have pointed
out how greatly he was indebted to the Church for his notions
about the art of ruling. None the less, forming an exception
almost unique in history, he was the undisputed master alike
of the spiritual and of the temporal power. His personality
was at once so outstanding and so permeated with the Christian
ideal that he was able to impose himself without effort on
clerics, bishops and the very Papacy itself. None of his contemporaries seems to have taken offence at this. Charlemagne
nominated bishops, made rules for admission to monasteries,
prescribed fasts, called synods together and examined their
decisions. In defiance of the Pope, who was anxious not to
quarrel with the Greeks, he insisted on the *Credo* being sung
at Mass, with the addition of the *Filioque*. In dogmatic controversies, concerning such matters as "adoptianism and the
cultus of images", he spoke in a tone of command and saw
that his decisions were put into effect. He was equally concerned
about disciplinary matters, reminding priests of their duty of
living in accordance with the sacred canons, monks of their
obligation to act in conformity with St. Benedict's Rule. The

*Missi Dominici* were instructed to look into all the details of the Christian life, to make sure that religion was being properly observed. Were the rules governing the Liturgy and those of the Sacred Chant being properly observed? Did the people know their prayers? Were they still addicted to pagan practices? Were the priests leading private lives worthy of their vocation? Such were the questions to which answers had to be supplied.

The Holy See itself was not exempt in practice from the Imperial tutelage. After the election of Leo III (795), Charlemagne's envoy, Angilbert, recalled to the Pope—on his master's behalf—that he was bound to lead a pure life, to observe the Sacred Canons, to govern the Church in an edifying manner, and to fight heretics:

> Our own task [added the Imperial message] is, with the aid of Divine goodness, to defend the Church of Christ externally against the incursions of pagans and the ravages of infidels; and to strengthen it internally by the diffusion of the Catholic faith. Your task, Holy Father, is to help us in our fight, by raising your hands towards God like Moses, in order that, through your intercession, the Christian people may be always and everywhere victorious over the enemies of His Holy Name.[12]

To put it shortly, prayers were considered to be the Pope's business, whilst the active protection of the Church, both in the spiritual and temporal sphere, devolved upon Charlemagne. Conscious of his power, the Emperor liked to assume the name of David in the select literary circle of which Alcuin was the leading spirit; he also, with reference to his religious reforms, assumed the name of King Josias. Certainly no sovereign was ever in a position to assume more appropriately the names of the great Biblical monarchs.

An author of his own day, the Carolingian priest Cathwulf, even took pains to find a theological reason for this pre-eminence of the King of the Franks. In an anonymous treatise of the patristic epoch may be read this brief observation: "The King is in the image of God as the Bishop is in the image of Christ";[13] and Cathwulf, writing to Charlemagne in about 775, found it easy to deduce from this text the doctrine of the supremacy of the King over the Episcopate. "Remember always, with fear and with love, the God who is thy King and of whom thou art the representative, in order to guard and to govern the members (of His Church). . . . The Bishop comes in the second place; he is only the representative of Christ."[14] By likening the relations between the Father and the Son in the Blessed Trinity to the relations between the Royal dignity and the Episcopate, Cathwulf cleared the way for future upholders of Caesaro-papism: an achievement which entitles him at least to this cursory mention.

The spiritual dictatorship of Charlemagne is an isolated phenomenon in his own century. It was only his incomparable personality which made it possible for him to dominate for a short time a Church which at that time was an incarnation of all culture and whatever was best in civilization. His successors had neither the strength, nor indeed the opportunity, to follow his example, and so things remained until the overthrow of the Carolingian dynasty.

From the end of the tenth century the German Emperors in their turn tried to renew the tradition of Justinian. They partially succeeded, going so far as to nominate bishops, found abbeys, and provide for St. Peter's Chair Popes of their own choice. Even the pious Emperor Henry II was here no exception. His undeniable reforming zeal, says M. Auguste Fliche, did not prevent him from "remaining faithful to the tradition of Caesaro-papism handed down to him by his predecessors. He considered himself to be, as it were invested in the Church with a supreme power of direction and correction."[15] But this new temporal domination over the Church was not to last for much more than a century and would be brought to an end by Gregory VII in the dispute over the investitures.

From this time forward and up to the end of the Middle Ages, the Empire and the young national monarchies were involved in various embittered conflicts with the Church. They did not however win any victory decisive enough to establish the religious supremacy of the secular power. The Empire, of which Barbarossa and Frederick II had tried to maintain the prestige, broke up in 1250 and never enjoyed for the future more than a diminished splendour. The national

4*

monarchies, for their part, were fully occupied in protecting their nascent sovereignty against the might of the Church and the encroachments of the feudal lords. It was thus impossible for them to think as yet of restoring the domination over the clergy of a Charlemagne or a Byzantine emperor. Actually, it was perhaps the petty German princes of the fifteenth century who achieved the greatest measure of success in this direction. Fortified by numerous Papal concessions, some of them seemed to be in a position to make their own the boast attributed to the Duke of Cleves: *Dux Cliviae est papa in terris suis*.[16]

*     *     *

Even though largely neutralized during the Middle Ages by the pre-eminence of the Church, the theory of Caesaro-papism was nevertheless defended during this period by a series of able writers. These works, now almost unknown, preserved the tradition and even succeeded, by means of specious arguments, in increasing its appeal. During the Investitures conflict, the defenders of the royal power laid tremendous emphasis on the significance and on the symbolism of the coronation ceremony. Guy of Osnabrück compared it to the priesthood. "The King," he wrote, "is rightly distinguished from laymen since by his unction with consecrated oil he becomes a participant in the sacerdotal ministry."[17] Guy de Ferrace (1086) compared the King to Moses and claimed that the functions which he had to fulfil were even more sacred than those of priests:[18]

> Let those who think that the ordinations of the Churches belong to priests, vouchsafe to consider that Moses was not a priest. Nevertheless God placed him over the people of Israel and granted him so high a position of honour that it was through him that He transmitted the Law, through him that He created and ordained priests; through him that He made known what sacred objects, what ministers, functions, rites, what sacrifices appropriate to divine worship were to be set aside for His Temple. Now if all these things were granted to Moses who had not himself any sacred function, how can it appear unworthy that the ordinations of the Churches take place by order of Emperors and of Kings, those

who at their coronation have received functions holier in certain respects than those of the priests themselves?

A little later, at the beginning of the twelfth century, certain defenders of the royal authority in England revived the arguments of the priest Cathwulf, appealing in this connexion to the mysteries of the Blessed Trinity and of the Incarnation. Thus we may note that, in a treatise dedicated to King Henry I (1103), the monk Hugues de Fleury wrote as follows: "The King in his kingdom seems to be an image of the Father Almighty and the Bishop an image of Christ. It follows from this that all the Bishops of the Kingdom must submit to the King, as the Son submits to the Father, not because of his nature but because of his rank. In this way the Kingdom as a whole is seen as a single unit."[19] Another writer of the period, the anonymous author of the *Tractatus Eboracenses*, bases his whole argument on the two natures of the Incarnate Word:

> Christ is God and man, true priest and true king in an eminent degree. As King, He is God Eternal, Uncreate, equal to His Father and One with Him. He is Priest through having been clothed with our humanity; in this quality He was appointed according to the Order of Melchisedech, was created, and is inferior to the Father . . . It follows that, in Christ, the royal power is greater than the priestly power, that it takes precedence over it just as the divinity takes precedence over the humanity. It is for this reason that some consider that amongst men the royal power is superior to the priestly power, because it is in the likeness of the higher nature of Christ and of His divine power. In consequence, they add, it is not contrary to God's Justice that the sacerdotal dignity should be established by the royal power and should be subject to it. Christ has in fact been appointed priest thanks to His royal power; He is subject to His Father in virtue of His priestly power, but He is equal to Him in virtue of His royal power.[20]

That the author shares the view given above is made clear by the whole tenor of his treatise. Indeed he is so pleased with his argument that he returns to it several times with obvious satisfaction. It must be admitted that he puts his case very cleverly. He supernaturalizes the royal dignity by linking it

up with the Kingship of Christ, making sure by this means of
its preponderance over the priesthood. We can see from this
how dangerous it is to gloss over the difference between royal
and spiritual authority; this is a process which ends in the
palliation of every encroachment and in a general blurring of
principles. The remarks of the monk of Fleury and the anonymous theorist of York were not destined to remain unheeded.
Wycliff, "the morning star of the Reformation", adopted them
in the fourteenth century and based upon them very daring conclusions in favour of the King's domination over the Church.[21]

The defenders of the regalist theory, in the France of Philip
the Fair, were content with arguments of a less bizarre character. It was to the Old Testament that they turned in order to
find illustrious examples which they could set before the King.
We may mention especially two works of this period which
defend with conviction theories verging upon Caesaro-papism.
The *Dialogue du clerc et du chevalier* (*c.* 1302) which claims to be
defending the true interests of the nation, maintains that the
Prince has a right to control the Church and to ensure that
good use is made of the donations made to her. The author
quotes in favour of his thesis the example of King Josias, the
reformer of the clergy.[22] Another anonymous treatise, *Rex
Pacificus*, makes even more effective use of the history of Israel,
contrasting the absolute power of Moses, temporal Head of
the Chosen People, with the secondary rôle of Aaron, who is
merely charged with the conduct of Divine worship. "It is
certain," continues this author, "that the Kings of those days
presided over temporal affairs, the priests and prophets over
spiritual affairs. Never in those times were priests or prophets
known to give orders to the King, as though possessed of any
authority to rule. . . . Kings on the other hand, being the true
lords and masters, commonly gave orders to priests and prophets."[23] Indeed, once Moses, David, Ezechias and Josias had
made it clear who were the "supreme masters", the priests
and prophets never attempted to do anything which could
diminish to the smallest extent their temporal power.[24]

It is only, however, when we come to Marsilius of Padua,
a professor at the University of Paris, that we find the true
source of the tradition of Caesaro-papism. It was during the

course of the conflict between Pope John XXII and the
Emperor Ludwig of Bavaria that he drew up his great political
work, the *Defensor Pacis*. A fervent disciple of Aristotle, Marsilius
saw clearly that, in the Aristotelian scheme of things, the
organization of worship, like that of the army and of the police,
was a function of the State; that no spiritual society could enjoy
real autonomy *vis-à-vis* the temporal power. He concluded that
the Christian State could not, in this respect, be inferior to its
pre-Christian prototype. Whilst not going so far as to deny the
divine origin of the Church, he refused her all independent
jurisdiction, even in matters spiritual. The Church did not in
his eyes constitute any distinct spiritual body; she was no more
than an aspect of political society, and her hierarchy was simply
a corps of magistrates. On these premises he was free to teach
the universal jurisdiction of the State—the Church depended
on it, he averred, alike in her disciplinary and in her administrative capacity. It was for the State to choose candidates for
ordination to the priesthood, to appoint priests to their respective parishes, to nominate bishops and to control diocesan
administration. Without the Prince's authorization, no decision
could be taken concerning the sacred rites, days of fasting and
of abstinence, Church holidays. All coercive action, notably
the excommunication of heretics and the initiation of pro-
ceedings against them, also lay in the hands of the secular
authority. Even the calling of General Councils was regarded
as being within the competence of the Emperor, "the supreme
human lawgiver".[25]

In spite of their having been so largely dominated by the
influence of the Church and the prestige of the Papacy, the
Middle Ages in the West did therefore play a part of manifest
importance in the history of Caesaro-papism, its doctrine and
its realization. This renaissance, in such unfavourable circumstances, of ancient ideas about the State helps us to understand
how remarkably vigorous and tenacious they were. We are
accordingly less surprised to note that, with the outbreak of
the Reformation crisis, these ideas made an aggressive reappearance upon the stage of a now long Christian Europe.

*          *          *

The triumph of Caesaro-papism in the Protestant kingdoms and principalities was an immediate result of the religious revolution.

In England, the first act of Henry VIII, after his rupture with the Holy See, was to have himself proclaimed by both Houses of Parliament "Sole Supreme Head of the Church of England" (November, 1534). In this capacity, ran the Law, the King had full power to "visit, repress, redress, reform and amend all such errors, heresies, abuses, contempts and enormities which by any manner of spiritual authority might lawfully be reformed". Thus it was that every right hitherto belonging to the Pope was transferred to the King. The dues paid by the clergy to the Holy See were now seized by the Crown, which took over all legislative authority in spiritual matters, nominating bishops and acting as supreme court of appeal in ecclesiastical causes, whilst it arrogated to itself the right to fix doctrine after consultation with the bishops. As Chapuys, Charles V's ambassador in England remarked, Henry VIII had become in truth "King, Emperor and Pope within his kingdom".[26]

Abrogated by Mary Tudor in 1554, the Act of Supremacy was revived by Elizabeth soon after she ascended the throne. The title of "Supreme Head of the Church" which Henry VIII had assumed was altered by his daughter to that of "Sole Supreme Governor of this Kingdom, as well in things spiritual and ecclesiastical as in things temporal". The Queen made immediate use of her spiritual power by pushing through Parliament the Act of Uniformity which transformed public worship and restored, with some modifications, the Prayer Book of Edward VI's day. Thus the dual sovereignty, civil and religious, of the Kings of England was firmly and enduringly established.

As might have been predicted, there was no lack of theorists to justify, in the face of public opinion, a revolution even so radical as this. Certain medieval works here served a useful purpose, and were at once drawn upon, some for quotation, some to provide arguments. In about 1534, as M. Pierre Janelle has pointed out, a whole series of treatises and small works set out to explain the legal grounds for the royal seizure of spiritual power; and it was now that English translations appeared of

*Defensor Pacis* of Marsilius of Padua, and of *Le Dialogue du
Clerc et du Chevalier.* The most important original work published
at this time was the *De vera obedientia* by Stephen Gardiner,
Bishop of Winchester, in which he drew largely upon the
example of the biblical kings and the legislation of the Emperor
Justinian. Here also is to be found the following important
proposition of which the defenders of the Reformation were in
future to make so much use: the Church is no more than an
amalgam of functions analogous to those proper to the practice
of medicine or to a university; this being so, she must be entirely
subject to the King's will. It would not seem that any use was
made by this writer of the theological arguments put forward
by Wycliff or the anonymous divine of York. These had not,
however, been forgotten, at any rate they reappeared in a later
work by an Anglican theologian, the *De suprema potestate regia*
of Ralph Abbot. It may be noted in passing how this writer
justifies the authority of the Prince over the Church indepen-
dently of the possession of Sacred Orders. Just as in the Trinity,
he says, the Father issues commands and the Son puts them
into execution, so the King, as vicar of God the Father, gives
orders which are executed by the bishops as vicars of Christ
in virtue of the Sacred Orders with which they are endowed.
It is not for the King to confer the Sacraments but he issues
commands to the ministers who have received the power to
do so.[27] Thus we find the theologians themselves reassuring
the Prince as to the lawfulness of his jurisdiction.

In the German principalities, too, the victory of Caesaro-
papism followed upon the religious revolution as an inevitable
consequence. Apparently Luther began by drawing an extremely sharp distinction between Church and State. According
to his view, the true Church was invisible; it was not a human
organization which could enter into competition with the civil
power, but was formed of true believers only and owned no
authority at all save that of Christ—the State, on the other hand,
had only a temporal and secular vocation, it only possessed the
powers of a policeman. In fact this separation was, however, but
an illusion, a mere abstraction. If, as the Lutheran theory maintains, every Christian is in fact a priest, the Prince participates

in the priesthood as do all other believers. "We cannot therefore," Luther himself concludes, "refuse him the title of priest and bishop, or the privilege of considering his charge to be a *spiritual* function, Christian in character and useful to the entire community."[28] What is more, the absence of a visible Church, possessing a real authority of its own, means that the functions of organizing worship and of appointing and supervising ministers remain unfulfilled. Who should then take over these functions except the Prince, the leading member of the *Corpus Christianum*? So it is that the reformer himself supplies the justification for the subjection of worship and religious discipline to State control.

Luther well realized, none the less, the danger of an arbitrary exercise of power which the position in the Church now assumed by the Prince would involve. In the early days he tried to deflect this danger by only allowing a limited right of intervention to the sovereign. But the ambition of the secular authorities and the pressure of events were too much for him and, in order to avoid the social troubles stirred up by the Anabaptists and to restore a *morale* which had been greatly sapped by the religious revolution, he had to overcome his initial hesitation and to bestow upon the sovereign what Melanchthon was to call the "two tables of the Decalogue". By 1525 he was requesting the Elector of Saxony to organize the visitation of the Churches. That potentate, as we can well imagine, was only too eager to act upon this request, and in the "Instruction to the Clergy" which he drew up in 1527 he clearly manifested his intention of exercising henceforth a dual control, religious as well as civil, over his principality. "With this Instruction," writes a Protestant historian, Herr Karl Holl, "the royal authority over the Church became a reality."[29] The other Protestant Princes painstakingly followed an example backed by such authority, and so in Lutheran Germany the system of State Churches came to be generally accepted.

The future was to show only too clearly to what lengths the secular authority would push its hold over religion. The Prince was not content to administer ecclesiastical property, to nominate pastors and to maintain discipline. He soon became the arbiter of the faith. The *Jus Reformandi* which was recognized at the Peace of Augsburg (1559) allowed him to settle the national religion and to force his subjects to accept it, under pain of banishment. This was the principle which was to be expressed later in the celebrated formula: *cujus regio, ejus religio.* As in England, so in Lutheran Germany, the dawn of modern times saw Caesaro-papism revived in its most extreme, its most oppressive, form. In Christian antiquity, the religious absolutism of the Caesar was never able to spread beyond certain limits; it always in the end found its way barred by the resistance of the Church. But in the Protestant States and principalities of the sixteenth century, no antidote of this kind was available. After fifteen centuries of Christianity the modern world tried to resuscitate the ancient notion of the all-powerful State.

With the exception of Calvin, who resolutely aimed at a clerical theocracy, the great protagonists of the Reformation shared Luther's ideas as to the quasi-episcopal power of the Prince. Melanchthon, Brenz, Zwingli, Bucer, Rhegius and Capito were not satisfied with the bestowal upon him of the right to preserve external discipline, they insisted that it was his royal duty to punish heretics; to propagate the new religion, even by violent means; and to abolish "idolatry", that is to say, the Holy Mass and Catholic worship. In order to stir up the royal zeal, they recalled to mind the example given by Old Testament Kings, and they likened his office to that of a *paterfamilias* who looks after the spiritual as well as the temporal needs of his children. "The Prince," concluded Capito, "is a shepherd, a father, the visible head of the Church upon earth. Christ is the true and natural Head of the Church . . . He has given to godly princes the gift of rule, bestowing on them at the same time the prudence which they need to govern in a godly manner: and it is because of this that he has decreed that one of them should be the head of each of his Churches in this world."[30]

After some years' experience, there was no denying the grave inconveniences, from a religious point of view, of the new system. About 1560, an unquestionably loyal Protestant, Flacius Illyricus, expressed his disappointment in bitter words:[31]

If once the Roman Pontiffs encroached upon the authority of temporal sovereigns, to-day it is the princes and civil magistrates who encroach upon the authority of the Church. These men arm themselves with both swords although they are scarcely capable of wielding the one to which they in fact have a right . . . The result is that, instead of a single Pope, we to-day have a thousand, that is to say, as many as we have princes, magistrates and great lords, all of whom now exercise, either at once or turn by turn, ecclesiastical and civil functions, arming themselves with the sceptre, the sword and spiritual thunderbolts, in order to dictate to us even what doctrines we must preach in our churches.

But these vigorous protests remained, as was inevitable, without repercussions—for the temporal sovereigns who had so unexpectedly regained possession of their ancient power, had not, we may be sure, the least intention of ever abandoning it again.

The sensational reaction in favour of Caesaro-papism which took place in the countries where the Reformation triumphed made the analogous tendencies observable in the realms that remained Catholic seem, by contrast, mild indeed. Such tendencies none the less existed, smiled upon by a nationalism which was steadily growing more exacting and more suspicious. They could be met with in Spain where the Catholic Kings showed themselves to have a remarkable gift for extorting from the Holy See the most astonishing spiritual concessions; they could also be noted in France, where the monarchy exerted a marked and steadily increasing sway over the national clergy.

Nationalism again, based as it was on the new political doctrines, was to give birth, little by little, to the laicized varieties of Caesaro-papism. It paved the way for a new political system, increasingly indifferent to religion for its own sake, but all the more exacting in matters touching sovereignty. This movement in favour of the lay State did not only affect Catholic countries; it also made itself felt in Protestant States. The latter continued to govern the Churches but did not attach any particular importance to their religious functions. The administration of ecclesiastical affairs was, in the rulers' eyes, only one aspect of their territorial sovereignty. After the sixteenth century, the supremacy of the State over the Churches, far from diminishing, increased greatly. We can no longer call it Caesaro-papism, however, for it had ceased to be inspired by that sense of a religious mission by which Justinian, Charlemagne and even the Byzantine emperors had been so much influenced. Nor had it any longer anything to do with the idea of a spiritual vocation which the early Reformers had associated with Christian princeship. It no longer stood in fact for anything but what we may call, in the full sense of the term, unbridled domination. And so it was that the formula characteristic of the new epoch—modern regalism—to which we shall devote more attention later on—appeared upon the scene.

Before it became—as we have said—laicized, Caesaro-papism had already constituted for centuries a sore temptation to Christian princes. A specious temptation, because it was capable of arising out of a sincere devotion to the interests of religion. A very dangerous temptation, none the less. For not only was Caesaro-papism bound to lead to conflicts with the spiritual power, it also was of grave detriment to authentic Christianity in that it entrusted the care of religious matters to an extraneous authority with no genuine mission. It cannot be too often repeated that the State, even the Christian State, has only a temporal authority; it never received from Christ a particular vocation to lead souls directly into the way of salvation.

As an historic experiment, Caesaro-papism contains a valuable lesson for us. It seems to prove in fact that it is very difficult to safeguard the duality of power when the territorial boundaries of a Church coincide with those of a State. The Church can then no longer compensate for her physical weakness by any extension of her spiritual domain. Confined within the frontiers of one State she lacks prestige; sooner or later, she will inevitably be absorbed by her too close and too powerful partner. This is obvious in the case of the Oriental Church, for the fact of her having elected, at the expense of her link with Rome, to become more and more self-sufficient, only resulted, in the end, in her becoming a mere tool in the hands of the Byzantine Empire. All the self-governing schismatic Churches have shared the same fate: in their capacity as national Churches they have been obliged to hand themselves over completely to the tender mercies of the temporal power. The same must be said of the Anglican and Lutheran Churches; reduced to government departments of the State or principality —*cujus regio, ejus religio*—they became quite incapable of resisting the hegemony of the Prince and his despotic absolutism. The real and effective distinction between the spiritual power and the temporal power is, in practice, only possible with a strong and organized Universal Church. She alone can preserve *vis-à-vis* the national authority her prestige and her liberty of action. She alone can give to spiritual sovereignty a majesty which commands respect.

## NOTES TO CHAPTER VI

[1] II Sam. vi. 17; xxiv. 25; I Kings vii. 14, 55; ix. 25.
[2] II Kings xxii–xxiii.
[3] II Paral. xxvi. 16–21.
[4] Palanque in the *Histoire de l'Eglise* (Martin et Fliche), III, p. 65. Battifol, *La Paix Constantinienne*, Paris, 1914, p. 352.
[5] St. Athanasius, *Historia Arianorum*, c. 33. Cf. Battifol, *op. cit.*, p. 472.
[6] In the *Corpus Juris Civilis;* see also Epistle No. 123: cf. K. Voigt, *Staat und Kirche von Konstantin dem Grossen bis zum Ende der Karolingerzeit*, Stuttgart, 1936, pp. 44–58.
[7] Battifol, *Cathedra Petri*, Paris, 1938, pp. 278–279.
[8] Tondini edition (Russian text and French translation), Paris, 1874, p. 2.
[9] Texts quoted by M. Jugie, *Theologia dogmatica Christianorum orientalium ab Ecclesia Catholica dissidentium*, Paris, 1931, IV, pp. 559 *et seq.*
[10] S. Ambrose, *Epist.* XX, No. 8 and 19. *Contra Auxent.* No. 36; *Patrol. Lat.*, XVI, 997, 999, 1018.
[11] Migne, *P.L.*, LXXXIX, c. 521–522.
[12] Mon. Germ. Hist., *Epist.*, IV, pp. 137–138.
[13] *Quaestiones in veteri et novo Testamento* (Ambrosiaster); *P.L.*, XXXV, 2234.
[14] Mon. Germ. Hist., *Epist.*, IV, p. 503.
[15] A. Fliche, *L'Europe Occidentale de 888 à 1125*, Vol. II of the *Histoire du Moyen Age* published by G. Glotz, Paris, 1930, p. 245.
[16] J Hashagen, *Staat und Kirche vor der Reformation*, Essen, 1931, pp. 550–557.

[17] Mon. Germ. Hist., *Libelli de Lite*, I, p. 466.

[18] *Ibid.*, I, p. 566.

[19] *De Regia potestate et de sacerdotali dignitate*, I, 3; Mon. Germ. Hist., *Libelli de Lite*, II, p. 468.

[20] Mon. Germ. Hist., *Libelli de Lite*, III, 667.

[21] *De Officio Regis*, C.1 and 6; Pollard, London, 1887, pp. 13 and 137.

[22] M. Goldast, *Monarchia S. Imperii Romani*, Hanover, 1611, I, pp. 15–16.

[23] M. Dupuy, *Histoire du différend d'entre le Pape Boniface VIII et Philippe le Bel*, Paris, 1655, p. 673.

[24] In regard to these two works, cf. J. Rivière, *Le Problème de l'Eglise et de l'Etat au temps de Philippe le Bel*, Paris, 1926, pp. 252 *et seq.*

[25] *Defensor Pacis*, published by Scholz, Hanover, 1932, *passim*.

[26] G. Constant, *La Réforme en Angleterre*, Vol. I, Paris, 1930, pp. 66–67.

[27] R. Abbot, *De suprema potestate regia*, London, 1619, pp. 20 and 30.

[28] *To the Christian Nobility* (1520).

[29] K. Holl, *Gesammelte Aufsätze zur Kirchengeschichte*, Vol. I, "Luther", p. 378.

[30] Text quoted by N. Paulus, *Protestantismus und Tokranz im 16 Jahrhundert*, Freiburg-im-Breisgau, 1911, p. 140, n.l. Numerous texts to this effect, drawn from the works of the principal reformers, can be found in this book.

[31] Dedicatory epistles of the 4th and 5th centuries, quoted in Döllinger, *Die Reformation*, II.

# VII

# CLERICALISM

CAESARO-PAPISM was a solution consonant with a phase of history that has now vanished. No contemporary government claims to be the guardian of the Church's discipline or the arbiter of the Faith. It is thus possible to view with philosophic detachment a theory which can to-day number but few adherents. Much importance is, on the other hand, attached by our contemporaries to questions connected with clericalism, and in any study of the relations between Church and State, this topic deserves a place. We will enquire then, as objectively as possible, whether there has ever existed, or still exists, as a result of certain tendencies in the Church, anything that can be termed a "clerical danger".

Invented towards the end of the French Second Empire and popularized by Gambetta—"*le clericalisme voilà l'ennemi*"—the expression spread like wildfire. It became the slogan of all the conflicts about education and religion which occurred under the Third Republic. Like all expressions with a polemical background, this tendentious term, at first aimed at the political action of the clergy, acquired a wider meaning and came to be extended later to every phase of the Church's life. If we were to be guided by propagandist literature, we should have to describe all priestly activity, apart from that concerned directly with Divine worship, as "clericalism". The moral and spiritual apostolate of the laity is likewise suspect; in the eyes of its enemies, Catholicism is transformed into clericalism directly it extends its interest to matters other than services in church and interior devotion. Thus, when the Church's moral influence on public opinion or on the State authority is in question, we hear the cry of *clericalism*! When the social work of the Church is mentioned or the intervention of Catholics in matters connected with workers or trades unions, again it is *clericalism*! The educational work of the Church is, of course, a manifestation of *clericalism*, as is the purely spiritual apostolate under its modern name of "Catholic Action"! It is apparently regarded as an offence against the lay State to form Catholic *élites* in professional circles, and some pre-war scribblers even denounced as "clerical" propaganda the fight against pornography and the campaign of the *Ligue féminine* against immorality on bathing beaches.

Under the name of clericalism, it is often Catholicism itself that is attacked, its social and hierarchial character, its spiritual influence. On the lips of the Church's enemies the significance of the word clericalism is indefinitely widened until it becomes co-extensive with the true Faith of Christ which is however grossly caricatured. This being so, we can better appreciate the reason for a certain admonition addressed by Pius XI to various misguided souls who genuinely imagined "not only that they could be Catholics without being clericals, but that they could even indulge in anti-clerical activities without thereby acting against the Church". *Intelligenti pauca*, was the Pope's comment on such people[1] and it is in fact only too clear that those who attempt to draw such distinctions are falling into a trap set for fools. For unscrupulous enemies of the Church are capable of making their simple-minded allies perceive the "clerical danger" here, there and everywhere.

We need certainly not, however, conclude from the above that the existence of clericalism is a figment of the imagination; for, as Mgr. Sagot du Vauroux has written, "those who wield religious authority have been known to advance exaggerated pretensions, thus giving a handle to critics and provoking the hidden or avowed hostility of what is called 'anti-clericalism'."[2] It is pretensions and attitudes such as these which we shall now attempt to describe. In this way we shall give the word "clericalism" a more exact meaning and one entirely freed from polemical presuppositions. The word is of recent origin, it is true, but the tendencies at which it strikes have been very noticeable since the Middle Ages. We should not be inclined to say that they are particularly marked in our own day. On the contrary—as we have seen—the action of the spiritual power has never appeared to be purer in its motives or more completely detached from political aims. In view however of persistent accusations, it is worth while to define a danger which the enemies of Catholicism delight to exaggerate, at the same time strangely distorting its significance.

In very general terms, one might define clericalism as the tendency of a Church or spiritual society to meddle in secular affairs with a view to making the State authority a mere instrument of its own designs. Such tendencies, we need hardly point out, have not made themselves felt amongst Catholics only. Protestantism, in its early days, provides us indeed with a famous example in the shape of the ecclesiastical dictatorship of Calvin at Geneva. This provides, beyond all doubt, the completest example of clerical predominance. It is true that the reformer never held any magistrature or sacred office. None the less, as an historian has justly remarked, "his words actuate the whole body politic and regulate its equilibrium down to the smallest details, from the faith to the fashions, and including both justice and foreign policy".[3] The temporal authority obsequiously echoed his decisions in every field; it was only the servant, the executor, of his will. Puritanism inherited from Calvin, its spiritual father, the same appetite for political power: and its temporal triumphs, in Great Britain and in America, were always assured by means of a clerical dictatorship of the most tyrannical kind. But let us return to the Catholic Church, whose long history makes it easy for us to pick out the temptations by which she has been assailed. One of the most specious and frequent of these temptations has been that of clericalism. When we examine it closely, moreover, it cannot simply be explained—as one might at first be inclined to imagine—by the undue prevalence of merely human motives. In fact, it is often seen to have been due to the general state of civilization, to the ideas prevalent at a given time or to the relations between the two powers. There are two sources for the danger which we are now considering. It is due, in large measure, to corruption and mixed motives on the part of the spiritual power, but it also can result from the structure of Christian society and from the principle on which the latter is based.

*          *          *

Regarded under its institutional aspect, the extreme form of clericalism would be represented by a Theocracy. This would mean a Christian society in which the ecclesiastical organization would totally absorb the State and its administration. The Pope would be Emperor of the world and the bishops his viceroys. Thus, the wheel having turned full circle, a totalitarian conception of the Church would take the place of the old totalitarian idea of the State. Such a fantastic dream, one need not point out, has never actually come true. Nor has any Pope ever thought of establishing such a régime, or of imposing it upon the world. Even the most powerful pontiffs, during the medieval period, never claimed to abolish, to their own profit, the all-important distinction between empire and priesthood.

That a danger of clericalism may nevertheless be discerned beneath the medieval structure of things, the preceding study on the primacy of the spiritual power has already shown. We there pointed out in what circumstances the Church became, during the Frankish epoch, the sole guide and director of Western civilization. There resulted from this a certain confusion between the Church and temporal society. First of all, indeed, the terms "Church" and "Christendom" might give a misleading impression and lead men to believe in the existence of two completely independent societies. We must recognize, in fact, that from the end of the ninth century, the word *Christianitas* is often used to mean the Christian world, the temporal order of Christendom, as opposed to the spiritual order, the ecclesiastical hierarchy, in a word, the Church. But in practice, such expressions were used very loosely and indiscriminately. Christendom, Mystical Body, Church, City of God: between the ninth and the thirteenth centuries all these terms were interchangeable, they were indeed barely distinguishable in the concrete, since all were expressive of diverse aspects of a single society, at once spiritual and temporal. The Pope was the Head of the Church, he also, if we consider the expressions used by Innocent III, claimed to be the Head and Foundation of Christendom. The Pope governed the Church; but the Emperor and the Kings governed it as well. Such, at any rate, was the notion prevalent in the Middle Ages and still current in the twelfth century, even in the writings of clerks. Thus we find Honoré d'Autun expressing the view that, so far as the government (*regimen*) of the Church in this present life is concerned, "the Lord has shown that two swords are necessary, the spiritual sword, which the priesthood wields against sinners, and the material sword of which the sovereign makes use to punish obstinate culprits".[4] The two swords! What endless controversies have sprung from the passage in the Gospel (Luke xxii. 38) which shows us the Apostles, during the Last Supper, presenting two swords to Our Lord! *Ecce duo gladii hic*! By the eleventh century the two swords had come to symbolize the two great powers of this world, and the problem of their relations with each other had given rise to controversies innumerable. On one point, however, all the disputants were agreed: both swords were within the Church. They symbolized, after their manner, the dual control. It was also stated, in the "Mirror of Saxony" (*Sachsenspiegel*) that the two swords ruled and defended Christendom.

This co-existence of the two swords, in the same Church, or Christendom, was one of the characteristics of the Middle Ages before the rise of the national monarchies. There were two distinct powers, two distinct hierarchies, the one civil and the other ecclesiastical; but there were not two independent and sovereign societies. The Pope and the Emperor, the Kings and the Bishops, did not rule over two radically different human communities; they were merely in charge of two distinct administrations within the City of God. In a Christendom thus regarded—M. Maritain has called it *une Chrétienté sacrale*—one can theoretically conceive of a collaboration between the civil and religious authorities in which there would be no confusion of the two powers or encroachments by the one on the preserves of the other. In practice, however, the danger of clericalism, once the spiritual power acquired great strength, could scarcely be denied. There is a considerable difference between the mutual relations of two sovereign powers and those of two administrative departments in the same organization.

The proximity and intimacy of two such departments is apt
to lead to mutual interference, especially by the stronger party.
This is precisely what happened with Church and State in the
Middle Ages. The ecclesiastics came to regard the temporal
power as a kind of vassal, or servant, who was there to carry
out menial tasks. Thus, about the middle of the twelfth century,
John of Salisbury did not hesitate to write: "The Prince is in
fact the servant of the Church; he performs that part of the
sacred functions which seems to be beneath the dignity of the
priesthood."[5] Innocent III declared, in similar language, that
the Sovereign Pontiff is the Head of the Church, the King is
only her right hand, "the secular arm". Some of the clergy,
as we have seen, went further than this and, under the pretext
of obtaining unity, attributed to the Pope the right to wield
both swords, likening the Prince to a mere vassal of the spiritual
power. This is the theory of the "direct power" which tends to
turn earthly sovereignties into mere fiefs of the Papacy.

We must in fact admit, at this period, the excessive power of
the ecclesiastical courts, the frequent interference of bishops
and of monks in civil affairs, the haughty tone adopted by
ecclesiastics when asserting their privileges. These facts can be
explained without difficulty, as we have already pointed out,
by the prolonged absence of the laity from the world of culture
and of civilization, a state of affairs which resulted in the Church
becoming, during what may be called the minority of the
European nations, their guide and maternal guardian. Only,
as so often happens with mothers and governesses, unaware of
the change that has taken place in their charges, she tried to
play this part for too long. The young nations were growing up
and clamouring for independence; and there was a danger that
the clerical tutelage to which they were still subjected might
end up as genuine clericalism. Conflicts broke out of which the
most sensational was the episode at the beginning of the fourteenth century which resulted from the rivalry between
Boniface VIII and Philip the Fair. Truth obliges us to admit that
some of the grievances of the royal authority in regard to
ecclesiastical privileges and immunities were by no means
imaginary.

Institutional clericalism has found itself opposed since the sixteenth century by the increase of royal authority and the revival of interest in the history of law. But no one had laid greater emphasis in his time than St. Thomas Aquinas on the secular character of temporal sovereignty. Taking as his foundation the *Politics* of Aristotle, he was bold enough to build upon it a solid theory of the temporal City, starting from human nature and its social needs. He thus restored to political society its natural origin and its autonomy. It was this Thomist and Aristotelian idea of the State which inspired certain theologians of his school, beginning with John of Paris, to formulate a new political doctrine which should safeguard anew the rights of temporal sovereignty. We find an echo of this tradition in the great encyclicals of Leo XIII, where there is nothing to remind us of the idea that Church and State are two subordinate departments of a single Christian power:

> In the same way as we find here below two great societies: the civil society, of which the immediate object is to procure for the human race goods of a temporal and terrestrial order, and the religious society whose aim is to lead men to their true happiness, to that eternal felicity in Heaven for which they were created; in the same way, there are two powers, subject both of them to the natural and eternal law and charged with providing, each in its own sphere, for the matters entrusted to their control . . . Each is sovereign in its own manner, each is contained within limits clearly defined and traced in conformity with its nature and its special aim. We have then, as it were, a circumscribed sphere in which each exercises its own activity *jure proprio*.[6]

Leo XIII spontaneously lights upon the very expressions used by Pope St. Gelasius at the end of the fifth century: the two powers are in the world (*in mundo*). He no longer declares, as was done in the Middle Ages, that these two powers are inside the Church (*in Ecclesia*). We therefore find clearly reaffirmed by the contemporary Papacy the autonomy of each power.

The sovereignty of the State, in its sphere, must form a solidly established basis for all Christian politics. It is dangerous to depreciate it, or to try to transform its nature. To do so, indeed, is to risk reintroducing the temptation of clericalism into spiritual society. This error, even in the modern epoch, can still lead men astray; it tends to make of civil society the servant and instrument of the Church. Towards the end of the sixteenth century, for example, certain theologians made use of the following comparison in order to describe the relationship between the two powers: "The situation of the State in regard to the Church is similar to that of the art of saddlery *vis-à-vis* that of equitation. These arts are different because their object and technique is different; however as the end of the first is subordinate to the end of the second, the one takes precedence of the other and dictates the rules it must follow."

Cardinal Bellarmine rejects this comparison in energetic terms:[7]

> It will not do at all. It is true that the inferior of the two arts above mentioned only exists because of the superior one. If the latter were not there, the former would have no point. If the art of equitation did not exist, the art of saddlery would be useless. Political power, on the other hand, does not derive its sole reason for existence from the ecclesiastical power. Even if the latter were non-existent, there would still be a political power, as happens in infidel lands where we find a real political and temporal power which has no particular relationship with a spiritual and ecclesiastical power.

We can see from this text how anxious Cardinal Bellarmine was to assure to the State full independence within its own sphere. He could not bring himself to consider the existence of political power to be, as it were, dependent upon that of its partner.[8] The offspring of man's social instincts, the temporal City, retains, in any event, its own existence and its particular end. Unfortunately the illustrious theologian did not push to its logical conclusion the radical distinction which he had drawn so convincingly, for, as we have already observed, his own conception of the "indirect power" practically restores to the Church, in certain exceptional circumstances, the temporal power which he elsewhere denies her.

Another formula exists, very fashionable at present, which —if wrongly understood—might be taken to favour clericalism. It is to the effect that, whilst the State is concerned with the *technical* aspect of things, the Church must deal with their *mystical* aspect. This theory can appeal in its own defence to certain declarations by the Popes and the hierarchy to the effect that the Church must not intervene in the "technical domain" or in questions of "political technique". It well expresses the determination of the Church not to enter into concrete problems of temporal organization: forms of government, questions connected with syndicates and trades unions, etc. It seems to us indispensable, however, that the opposition of these terms to each other should only be understood in a relative sense. Things "mystical" and things "technical" can never be radically opposed to one another in the way that spiritual and material things are opposed. The Church is a mystical power; she stands for an *ensemble* of beliefs, moral rules and means of sanctification; but she is also a visible society: her government and her administration are built upon a technical basis, of which the principles are formulated in the Code of Canon Law. The State, for its part, has a highly technical side, it concentrates and unifies under its direction a formidable array of organizations and public services. But it is not only a technical thing; we should be derogating from its sovereignty if we tried to restrict it to purely executive and administrative functions. The State, even the Christian State, cannot be compared to an auxiliary which receives from the Church all its moral directives and all its principles of government, nor should it be compared to a mechanician entrusted merely with the execution of technical arrangements. The State too has its *mystique*. By this word *mystique*—wrongly used perhaps but now generally accepted—we understand the characteristic shapes and tendencies which the human ideals of culture, justice and charity take upon themselves under different régimes. The *mystique* with which we are now dealing simply reflects in some degree the moral personality of the State, its character as a perfect society, provided, not only with a material organization, but with an ascending scale of moral and cultural values.

It is true that certain totalitarian *mystiques*, or ideologies, such as Nazism and atheistic Communism, have been formally condemned by the Church. At the other end of the scale it would be equally difficult to reconcile the anarchist or ultra-liberal ideologies with Catholic doctrine. Between these two extremes, however, there is room for a wide diversity of régimes and ideologies. It will doubtless not be forgotten that Pius XII in his Christmas message of 1944 clearly manifested his sympathy for the democratic ideal which, however, he took great care not to identify with the republican form of government, calling all States democratic in which a citizen can *in fact* "express his personal opinion about the duties and sacrifices demanded of him" and in which he cannot be "forced to obey without having been heard". He thus left us complete freedom of choice between many types of régime in which we can see combined, in varying degrees, liberty and authority, the traditional and the reforming spirit, popular action and governmental action. We should fall into "clericalism" if we were to advocate some particular political formula as being the only one that corresponded with the Church's ideas, the only one compatible with her mind. Such a manoeuvre as this would be as disquieting from the Church's point of view as from that of the State, for whilst it would endeavour to impose a particular ideology on the latter thus interfering with its sovereignty, it would involve the Church, for her part, in combinations and cliques which would have the most harmful effect on her mission. That political ideologies cannot leave the spiritual power indifferent we readily agree. Our present experiences suffice to reveal to us both their power of attraction and the appalling lengths to which their exponents can carry them. The Church is concerned with their activities and watches them closely, not with the object of choosing between them and of then imposing her choice, but in order to adapt her religious activity to present needs and, where possible, to place a check on any grave deviations. In any case, where her relations with adult nations are concerned, the Church should not be regarded as the custodian of a political ideology for the practical application of which she is liable to make the Christian Heads of State responsible.

Another form of clericalism would be to assign to the secular power too sublime an end and one disproportionate to its nature and to its temporal mission. The City, as such, is not there in order to ensure the eternal salvation of its members, it only has a terrestrial and a transitory rôle. Why should one think of imposing upon the moral personality of the State duties identical with those of an individual person? Why should one expect the State to fulfil all the prescriptions of Christian ascetics, beginning with the full observance of the law of abnegation and self-sacrifice? What should we say, for instance, of a sovereign who, in order to exercise his country in the virtue of humility, calmly involved it in one reverse after another? The reader will perhaps protest at this point and accuse us of frivolity; yet this is what M. Yves Simon wrote in 1934, in the course of a short essay on Christian politics:

> The history of St. Louis would be seen in quite a different light, were it to be interpreted by a more Christian notion of political prudence. We should then better realize that history is not composed merely of visible events but that invisible events are by no means the least important; we should understand that, from a Christian point of view, the translation of political prudence into historical facts by means of visible successes is purely accidental, and that, if we look at human destiny from a supernatural viewpoint, a Christian prince can be a perfect Head of State even though he has nothing to show to secular interpreters of history but a series of defeats. We should further take note that, from the very fact of its elevated purpose, of its readiness to act as an obedient instrument to divine grace, Christian political action is more likely than not, in the majority of cases, to be the reverse of brilliant. The Egyptian campaign would then take on a different significance and, contemplating St. Louis in the Mansourah Prison, preparing himself for the ashen bed of Tunis, we should recognize Christian political action in all its ideal excellence, completely stripped, absolutely purified and conformed to Christ the King.

Coming, as it does, to so paradoxical a conclusion, it is unlikely that the above theory of Christian politics will carry conviction. It is obvious that the conformity of the temporal with the spiritual is here pushed beyond permissible limits. No, the State is not assimilable to the Church to the extent of being bound of itself to achieve conformity with Christ Jesus. However lawfully established it may be, its sovereignty cannot aspire to a supernatural halo of this kind. Let us leave it in its own sphere, since, to borrow the very words of Pius XI, it is "necessarily confined within the boundaries of the natural, the earthly and the temporal"[9].

\*　　　　\*　　　　\*

We have hitherto considered the clericalist danger viewed as a result of misconceptions concerning the nature of the State and its sovereignty. In many cases, however, this danger arises less from what we can call a theory of government than from an instinctive tendency, it makes itself felt less in institutional ideas than in a propensity on the part of the clergy to promote the Church's reign by "carnal" and political means. In his book *Pax Nostra*, Père Fessard very aptly compares it to the Pharisaical spirit. The "carnal" and Pharisaical clerk, the "clerical" clerk, is, he says, one who, in his presentation of the Church and of her rôle in the world, gives preference rather to the formal, objective and visible elements in her life than to what is interior, spiritual and mystical.[10] In the time of Our Lord, the pride and narrowness of the Pharisees had coarsened and de-spiritualized the ancient religion of Israel, transforming it into an arsenal of rules and legal prescriptions. They had made it moreover into an instrument of political domination.

The promises of infallibility and of divine assistance did not mean that the Church would be saved from this danger and this temptation, but they did supply her with constant assistance in escaping from them. In certain centuries, for instance, too great an appetite for temporal goods was displayed by Churchmen; and, on the eve of the Reformation, the City of God assumed too many of the characteristics of a power of this world. The Church, even up to the time of Julius II, showed herself to be imperious, domineering, warlike; Papal policy bore a strange resemblance to that of the Italian princelings; the concession of indulgences and spiritual privileges took on the appearances of a financial enterprise. Some centuries later, shortly before the Revolution, the Church of France was an apparently solid and impressive institution. Wealthy and well

5

provided with benefices, here abbots and prelates cut an
imposing figure amongst the great ones of this earth. The first
of the Three Orders was a power in the land; but unfortunately
this was due far more to the earthly riches it possessed than to
any real ascendancy over souls. In Luther's day, and once more
at the end of the eighteenth century, a carnal mentality had
penetrated into the Church, tending to transform her religious
sovereignty into "clerical" domination. These were but passing
lapses, however, for which the splendid effort of the Counter-
Reformation and the devotion of the Church of the present to
her purely spiritual mission have more than compensated.
Nothing could be more revealing, in this connexion, than the
following observations made by Pius XI after the Lateran
Treaty and the cession to Italy of practically the whole of the
former Papal States:—"We are pleased to see the material
domain of the Holy See reduced to such narrow limits that one
can and must consider it as having been itself, so to speak,
spiritualized by the immense, sublime and truly Divine
spirituality which it is destined to champion and to serve."[11]

Another way in which the clergy can tend towards clericalism
is by seeking too readily the favour and support of the political
authorities. Loyalty towards the City of God, be it understood,
is not here at stake: for a long tradition of esteem and of profound
respect for the secular sovereignty exists in the Church and
dates from her earliest days. The exhortations of St. Peter and
St. Paul, the prayers for constituted authority in the Liturgy,
have inevitably served to confirm the Church in this attitude of
deference. In spite of this, she is fully aware of the precarious
and transitory character of every earthly government. Her desire
to live in harmony with the temporal power is therefore not
synonymous with an obsequious servility. It is tinged, indeed,
not with irony at the spectacle of ephemeral authority—as
M. Paul Claudel states somewhere[12]—but with a prudent and
discreet reserve. Nothing is, in any case, more harmful to her
spiritual interests, nothing is more calculated to arouse feelings
of prejudice and hatred against her, than the excessive attachment of her ministers to a man or to a régime. Uncalled-for
enthusiasm in welcoming a new government, indiscreet
endeavours to get into its good graces, a tendency to exaggerate

the obligations of loyalty towards it, can sometimes arouse
against the clergy resentments of the bitterest and most lasting
kind.

The French Second Empire supplies us with a memorable
instance of this. Following upon the social disorders of the
Second Republic, the dictatorship of the Prince-President was
welcomed with enthusiasm by a considerable proportion of the
clergy and of the episcopate. All went well during the early
years of the régime, when, doubtless to his own amazement, the
former *Carbonaro* heard himself compared in turn, by certain
members of the hierarchy, to Constantine, to Charlemagne and
even to St. Louis. But, in spite of appearances to the contrary,
the alliance was not destined to endure. Whilst still preserving
an outward semblance of respect, Imperial policy—particularly
after 1860—did all within its power to destroy the Church's
influence. It has even been described as the starting-point of
the religious conflicts which culminated in the Laws of 1901
and 1905. Now in all this train of events, the only episode that
remained fixed in the popular mind was the first; and in the
early days of the Third Republic the enthusiastic welcome given
by the clergy to the Empire provided anti-clerical agitators
with a favourite and inexhaustible theme.

Closer to our day, is it not a fact that certain ecclesiastics lost
all sense of proportion when they covered with adulation the
Vichy Government and its head? The fact that their behaviour
did not subsequently result in a fresh wave of anti-clericalism is
due solely to the refusal of the majority of the French clergy—
whose self-respect remained intact—to follow a bad example.

Broadly speaking, it is always dangerous for the Church to
link the cause of promoting God's Kingdom too closely with
political causes. It is of course perfectly legitimate for Catholics
to have their own personal preference for this type of government or that—and, should they endeavour, in their capacity
as citizens, to secure its triumph, no one can object to their
action as such, even though the means or occasion chosen may
perhaps leave scope for criticism. This would not be true,
however, if they were to enlist, on behalf of a secular enterprise,
the help and support of the religious authority. In such
circumstances the Church would find herself involved in a cause

which was not her own and her Ministers would be faced by the old temptation to which the elders of Israel succumbed. Ozanam, who in the closing days of the Second Republic was an anxious witness of attempts to commit the Church to manoeuvres of this kind, confided his fears in the following terms to his friend Dufieux:

> I see, dear friend, near at hand, a revival of the school of thought which confuses the interests of the Throne with those of the Altar; I see well-meaning men embracing anew the doctrines of the *Memorial Catholique* of 1824 and digging in advance the ravine into which the clergy would hurl themselves like a torrent, were it not that the Archbishop of Paris has barred their way with his Pastoral which has driven party-politicians to despair, but which will perhaps save Christianity in France next year, and which will at any rate redound to the credit of the Church in the sight of history . . .

Ozanam next went on to point out that all these intrigues for the purpose of obtaining the support of the Church for a new restoration themselves betrayed a lack of faith and an erroneous conception of the Christian Apostolate.

> Dear friend, we have not enough faith, we always desire to bring about the re-establishment of religion by political means, we dream of a Constantine who, all at once and by a single effort, will bring back the nations to the Fold. This shows how little we know about the history of Constantine, how he became a Christian merely because everyone was already more than half Christian, how the crowd of sceptics, indifferentists and parasites who followed him into the Church introduced into her Fold nothing but hypocrisy, scandal and lax tendencies. No, no, conversions are not brought about by laws, but by example, by the conquest, one by one, of individual consciences! . . . Do not let us ask God for a bad government, but do not let us either endeavour to provide ourselves with one that will dispense us from our duty, by taking upon itself a mission to the souls of our brothers with which God has not entrusted it . . . Let us continue, let us extend, our work of converting others, but let us hold in detestation that kind of weakness—that temptation to sloth and discouragement—which makes us call State proselytism to our aid!

It is possible that, in his desire to stress the all-importance of personal example, Ozanam here tended to depreciate unduly the effect of laws and institutions. The latter have their importance and may give effective support to spiritual forces. It is true, however, that the triumph of the Church can never be brought about by a simple change of régime or by a reform of the Constitution. Nor will it ever be achieved by the simple accumulation of laws and decrees. Progress in legislation must in this field take seriously into account the general level of manners and the state of men's minds. It must accompany spiritual progress and not go rashly on ahead. It is impossible to convert a de-Christianized society by means of decrees. The only result of these will in fact be to provoke anti-clerical reactions of the most virulent type.

The most notable example of this kind of thing is undoubtedly the law against sacrilege which, passed under Charles X in 1825, punished by death the profanation of the sacred vessels and of consecrated Hosts. In the first place, this law was in the nature of an anachronism, for it made the State directly responsible for punishing a crime of which the malice did not derive from the Natural Law but from the positive doctrine of the Church. In the second place the law proved to be most inopportune, for the Voltairean opposition, which was at that time so fierce, made unscrupulous use of it against the régime and against the "priests' party".

At the present day, when the de-Christianization of the masses has become so complete, the clergy and Catholic leaders must, in all their undertakings, bear this lamentable situation well in mind. There is nothing to be gained by radical and premature reforms of an institutional character. What, for instance, would be the effect of a sudden and complete restoration of Catholic instruction in the State schools? Undoubtedly a strong anti-religious agitation, most harmful to the Church and to her activities. No, it will be far more profitable to obtain for Catholic enterprises and Catholic teaching a real and unfettered liberty. The Christian apostolate will be able to make use of this to bring about a change of heart and to introduce, by slow stages, the necessary institutional reforms. "The Church does not win hearts by means of organizations," as M. Gilson has very justly remarked, "it is rather organizations that are won over by means of the heart."[13]

No study on the Church and politics would be complete without reference to another delicate question: that of Catholic political parties. One might imagine this to mean the political grouping of all the Catholics of a given country under the aegis of, and in direct dependence upon, the hierarchy. Such a notion would however be quite fantastic. It would be expressly contrary to the doctrine of the Church on the distinction of the spiritual and the temporal and would quite rightly incur the charge of clericalism. The principles on which the Catholic party in Belgium—for example—is based are entirely different. It is so called, says M. l'Abbé Riche, "because the members of the party profess the Catholic Faith and declare that, in governing the country, they will respect the Church's doctrine". But, as the Belgian bishops formally declared, in their pastoral letter of the 25th December, 1936, "the party cannot and does not claim for itself any mandate or commission from the Church", and the latter cannot be compromised by the political actions of the party.[14] The same no doubt applies to the other Catholic parties which existed at one time in Germany and in Italy. Founded for grave factual reasons, such as the need —in Germany—to counteract Protestant influences, these groups remained completely independent and were not subject, so far as purely temporal matters were concerned, to any control by the hierarchy.

It is none the less true that we can scarcely imagine in France the existence or the activities of a "Catholic party". The name disconcerts and embarrasses us; and the efforts which were made in about the year 1900 to form a party on these lines only raised suspicion and failed miserably. Without denying the success of such enterprises in other periods and in other countries, we note on this point that the whole idea is definitely distasteful to the French mind which would always see in it a danger of camouflaged clericalism.

*         *         *

Hitherto we have looked at the grievance known as clericalism under its essential aspect which is political in character, but we can also apply the term by analogy to all pharisaism, to every form of sclerosis or warping of the true conception of the Church's mission. The Church, the mystical Body of Christ, is also an external organization entrusted to men; and although she is assisted by the Holy Spirit, who will never allow her to degenerate and to deny her mission, she nevertheless has to defend herself against the insidious and coarsening effects of time and habit. If the clergy are not on their guard, there will be a danger of their control over men's souls becoming transformed in the end into tyrannical domination, of their watch over spiritual interests turning into routine administration, of their guardianship of the deposit of Revelation changing to suspicious traditionalism, of the certitude of Divine assistance degenerating into a proud self-sufficiency. The local and transitory appearance of this all too human tendency may well be said to embody that "clerical" spirit which sometimes harmfully affects the spiritual relationship of a priest and his flock. No one has better described this particular aspect of the aberration in question than Mgr. Pie, in a conference given to the clergy of his diocese:[15]

There are small faults which are more irritating than serious vices and which can easily prevent a priest from winning the merit which his fine qualities would otherwise deserve and from obtaining any results from his best work. Without striving after riches or power, one can, within the narrow bounds of one's pastoral activities and of one's personal reactions, fall into intolerably tyrannical ways. No, my dear brother, you are not the Mayor or his deputy, you are not a town-councillor, nor are you the treasurer or manager of a factory—you do not claim to hold any of these positions. But even though you do not aspire to any such dignities, it is said that you expect to be accorded, for your own sole advantage, all the privileges which they confer, that you encroach upon every one, that you monopolize everything, that you do not respect, or at least do not observe, any law, be it ecclesiastical or civil. It is also stated that you are imperious and domineering, that you do not accept any advice or any representation, that you follow your own inclinations . . . Let us put it plainly: if more prudence, more self-sacrifice, more humility, and a more Christian and priestly spirit had been shown, most of the local conflicts which have taken place during our political troubles would have been avoided.

Although grotesquely distorted for base polemical ends, the danger of clericalism is not then a pure myth, invented in its entirety by the Church's enemies. No Christian will be surprised at this. The Church has received from Christ the privilege of infallibility, in matters of dogma and morals; her leaders are not possessed of impeccability where questions of government and religious policy are concerned; they have been known to aim at securing, by unduly worldly means, the primacy of the spiritual power. Clericalism has at times been erected into a system; still more frequently, it exists in the shape of an instinctive tendency in the minds of all who might be inclined to aim at obtaining for the spiritual society an unduly conspicuous position of external domination. This danger has no doubt greatly diminished by reason of the difficulties which, in these days, are placed in the way of the Church's existence. It may, none the less, be still dreamt of as a possibility by certain theorists concerned with a revived Christendom. Distance lending enchantment to the view, the medieval system continues to have a seductive effect on certain imperfectly instructed minds; it fills them with nostalgia for the golden age of the Church and for the Christian civilization of the Middle Ages; they paint it in glowing colours and long for its return. Such persons forget, however, both the genuine weaknesses of the Church of those days and the circumstances which enabled it to act as it did, that is to say, the long slumber of secular culture and the fact that the Western nations had not yet come of age. We shall not be able to build a future Christianity by placing under the Church's tutelage powerful nations which have attained their majority. We shall not re-create a Christian civilization by reducing independent modern States to vassals of the Holy See. The methods of education suitable to children do not fit the mentality of the grown man. It is by means of the effulgence of her sanctity and of her spiritual *magisterium* that the Church will continue to carry out in this world her civilizing mission. It is by genuinely religious methods that she will extend her prestige and her influence over nations yet to be, freed from the deceptive mirages of a political supremacy or a "clerical" domination.

## NOTES TO CHAPTER VII

[1] Words of Pius XI on the 10th March, 1931, at an Audience given to the pupils and professors of the Angelicum (*Documentation Catholique*, 18 April, 1931, p. 958).

[2] *L'Eglise de France et la politique au temps présent*, Paris, 1936, p. 2.

[3] P. Mesnard, *L'essor de la philosophie politique au XVIe siècle*, Paris, 1936, p. 306.

[4] *Summa gloria*, 26; in Mon. Germ. Hist., *Libelli de Lite*, III, p. 75.

[5] *Polycraticus*, IV, 3; Migne, *Patrol. Lat.*; CIC, c. 516.

[6] Encyclicals *Immortale Dei* and *Nobilissima Gallorum Gens*.

[7] *De Romano Pontifice*, V, 6; *Opera Omnia*, Naples edition, 1872, I, p. 531.

[8] The classical analogy of soul and body cannot be unreservedly applied to this form of duality. The body, indeed, exists only by means of the soul and disintegrates directly the soul is withdrawn. The State, on the other hand, derives from the Church neither its existence, nor its maintenance in being.

[9] Encyclical *Non abbiamo bisogno* (29 June, 1931).

[10] *Pax Nostra*, Paris, 1936, p. 297.

[11] Address to Lenten preachers, 11 February, 1929, cf. *Documentation Catholique*, 23 February, 1929, p. 469.

[12] Preface to the posthumous book of Jacques Rivière, *A la trace de Dieu*, Paris, 1926, pp. 20–21.

[13] M. Gilson, *Pour un ordre Catholique*, Paris, 1934, p. 65.

[14] R. Riche, *Catholicisme et politique*, Brussels, 1937, pp. 28–30.

[15] *Entretiens avec le Clergé*, July, 1871, in Vigué, *Pages choisies du Cardinal Pie*, Paris, 1916, II, pp. 45, 47.

# VIII

# THE LAY STATE

As a result of the prodigious development of the young nations in the period which has elapsed since the sixteenth century medieval clericalism is now a thing of the past. The era of national imperialism succeeded, once the Reformation crisis was over, to the old Christian epoch which had now run its course. The modern State, influenced by the Renaissance, was gradually to adopt a new attitude towards spiritual affairs. In Protestant countries—with the exception of Geneva—the Reformers, in snatching the State from Catholic control, restored its complete autonomy, in spiritual as well as in temporal matters. They imagined, it is true, that the State would give its religious responsibilities pride of place over its secular mission, but they were completely deluding themselves; for the same movement caught hold, one after the other, of all the States of Europe; and whether Catholic, Lutheran, Anglican or Calvinist, all were involved though in differing degrees, in the same laicizing process. It is this complex and widespread phenomenon of which we must now analyse the origin and multiple aspects. Pernicious though it may have been in many respects, it would not be just to condemn it outright, allowing no appeal. Let us remember in the first place that Catholic doctrine permits a certain amount of State secularization. The laicist error, in political matters, did not consist in the stress it laid on the right to secularize the State; it consisted in the claim of the civil power to carry it to unlimited lengths, to make its own temporal interests the sole standard whereby its action should be determined. This error, as we shall see, can itself take two different forms corresponding with the character of the State concerned. Either the State claims to exercise a widespread control over the Church, affirming thus, in all domains of ecclesiastical life, the absolute nature of its sovereignty, in which case we have modern "regalism", the secular variant of Caesaro-papism. Or else, the State disinterests itself in the Church and abandons her to her fate, in so far as the Common Law allows, when we have Liberal Separatism. In the course of this intricate study of the evolution of political laicism, we have, whenever possible, chosen our examples from the history of France which is not only more familiar but also provides us with striking and characteristic episodes wherewith to illustrate the question under discussion.

## I. CAN THE SECULARIZATION OF THE STATE BE LAWFUL?

That it is really Christianity and the Christian doctrine about the civil power which lie at the root of the secular idea of the State may at first sight appear to be a paradoxical statement. Yet we need not spend much time proving its truth, for what we have already said about the Christian revolution has made it clear enough that Christ and the Apostles desired to maintain the secular character of the State and to deny it all competence in the spiritual domain. No such distinction was of course drawn in the ancient world, for there the Prince's authority extended alike over the sacred and over the profane, he was as much concerned with religious as with worldly affairs. In fact, even after the conversion of the Roman Empire, no real secularization of the State took place within the framework of Christian antiquity. It was not that the Church had forgotten her primitive teaching: bishops and popes, as we have seen already, had expressed themselves nobly and vigorously on the subject. But the Emperors were able to further their ambitions by turning to their own advantage the gratitude of churchmen. Compromises were accepted by the latter which in practice gave the Emperors important religious privileges, such as the right of convoking councils, of intervening in matters of Church discipline and even in controversies about doctrine.

The medieval period, up to the thirteenth century, was equally unpropitious to the idea of a lay State. The secular hierarchy and the ecclesiastical hierarchy did not at that time appear any longer to be administering two independent

societies, but the one and only City of God. They were both
dependent on the Church. In the conflicts which took place
between the priesthood and the royal or imperial authority, the
Prince's champions were wont to insist on the ecclesiastical,
nay, on the quasi-sacerdotal dignity of his office. Moreover,
despite these quarrels, the prestige of the Papacy and of the
clergy necessarily stood high in a civilization which owed its
inspiration essentially to the Church. Things remained thus
until the time when national sentiment in the West reached
maturity. This sentiment, which, however strong, was by nature
earthly and temporal, implanted in the European rulers a
completely secular notion of their mission, led to their adopting
a progressively independent line of policy towards the Holy See,
and inspired in their dependants an anti-clerical attitude of
mind. Boniface VIII was to issue a famous Bull on the subject,
the opening words of which would give candid expression to
the nature of his grievances: *Clericis laicos infestos.*

If we prescind from all the incidental excesses, there was
nothing that was not normal in this first secularization of the
temporal power—a fact which was clearly recognized, in the
reign of Philip the Fair, by certain ecclesiastics. Thus John of
Paris, whom we have mentioned above as a disciple of St.
Thomas Aquinas, laid stress on the priority of the State's
origin as compared with that of the Church; on its secular
origin deriving from the instinctive social needs of the human
creature; on its specifically temporal purpose, entirely distinct
from that of the spiritual society.[1] Hence, the difference in
nature between the two societies, which had been so strongly
felt in the Church in the days of pagan Rome, again impressed
itself upon men's minds. This doctrine was indeed to be
incorporated from this time forward in the Church's official
teaching and received in the encyclicals of Leo XIII and of
Pius XI—this has already been noted—the most complete
confirmation.

But if the political repercussions of patriotic sentiment brought
about, even during the medieval period, a partial secularization
of the State, Christendom still remained in being. It was not a
political power, strictly speaking, but rather a community
bound together by identical religious and cultural ties through

the existence of which the independence of the Western States was *de facto* limited. At the end of the fifteenth century the notion of Christian unity was still alive in Europe, enfeebled, no doubt, but still corresponding to a genuine need in men's hearts.

It was in the sixteenth century that the problem of State independence began to present itself under new forms, and the opening epoch of the modern period is of capital importance where the present question is concerned. How far in practice can a State be justified in secularizing itself? What must the limits of such secularization be, if reasonable harmony is to be preserved between Church and State? The replies to these intricate questions which are supplied by French political history are deserving, in our opinion, of particular attention, and by examining them we shall be enabled to substitute the considerations of definite cases which have actually occurred for mere abstract discussion. We may note, indeed, in French political life, two entirely distinct elements: on the one hand, measures of secularization necessitated by circumstances and not in themselves incompatible with spiritual interests; on the other hand, doctrines and new tendencies whence the idea of the modern lay State was eventually to be evolved. The study of these facts and theories will enable us to obtain a reasonably clear idea of modern laicism.

French political evolution was accelerated in the sixteenth century by an event of primary importance: the rupture of the ancient unity of Christendom beneath the assault of the Reformation and of the revolutions to which it gave rise. Protestantism separated England and the Scandinavian kingdoms from Rome and it divided into factions and warring principalities Germany, France, the Low Countries, Switzerland and Poland. The home and foreign policies of all these States were naturally affected by the repercussions of so immense a calamity.

Foreign policy, in the first place. For those Princes who had remained Catholic, the aim to be pursued seemed clear enough: a united front against the heretics and the restoration in Europe of the community of Christian nations. Indeed, public opinion in the Catholic countries spontaneously took this view, so deeply was the conviction of the need for spiritual unity ingrained in men's minds. In practice, however, the situation was much more complex. At the same time as the Reformation a new phenomenon had appeared in the West—the imperialist ardour of a great Catholic nation. Elected Emperor in 1519, heir to the Houses both of Austria and of Spain, Charles V resolved to transform into an objective reality the nominal dignity which had been conferred upon him. A fervent Christian, he was able to make use of his prestige as a Catholic sovereign to pursue an enterprise of unparalleled daring: that of obtaining universal domination alike over the old and the new worlds. A keen observer of the period, the historian François Guichardin, made no mistake about the situation:[2]

> One of the most fortunate things [he wrote] that can happen to a man is that he should be able to persuade himself that he is inspired by zeal for the public good to do those things which he does in his own interests. This is what rendered glorious the enterprises of the Catholic King. Carried out for the sake of his own security and greatness, they seemed to have no other aim than the propagation of the Christian Faith in the defence of the Church.

The same may be said of Philip II, his successor on the Spanish throne. From the time of the outbreak of the French wars of religion, he posed as the champion of Catholicism with the object of imposing upon the kingdom of France a kind of disguised vassalage. The Papacy, which was more far-seeing than a section of French opinion, was not taken in by this display of religious fervour. In the instructions addressed to Cardinal Caetani, the Legate of Sixtus V in France, regarding the settlement of the dynastic question (1589), we may read these acute reflexions:[3]

> The King of Spain as a temporal sovereign is above all anxious to safeguard and to increase his dominions and for this reason he will try to place at the head of the French State persons who are his creatures and to arrange things in such a manner that there will always be need of him and that he will be the arbiter and absolute sovereign. The preservation of the Catholic religion which is the principal

aim of the Pope is only a pretext for His Majesty, whose principal aim is the security and aggrandisement of his dominions.

Since Charles V's reign an immense ambiguity of purpose had oppressed Catholic Europe, for the projects to restore a united Christendom, so longed for by public opinion, had been transformed by the House of Austria into a detailed and realistic plan for its own secular domination. It was in order to ward off this acute danger that the Most Christian King had adopted a policy of secularization. In the course of his struggle against the Hapsburgs, he made use of reinforcements of which previous generations would have refused the assistance with horror: first, the Turks, and then the Protestant princes. It was in the very year of the calamity at Pavia that the first French ambassadors were sent to the Sultan, and from the celebrated capitulations of 1535 onwards, the Turkish alliance formed one of the essential factors in French foreign policy. Much the same may be said of the Protestant alliances. Unobtrusive and ephemeral to begin with, frequently broken off, during the period of the League or at the beginning of the reign of Louis XIII, as a result of reversals of policy, they became under Richelieu the characteristic feature of a system which amazes us by its modernity.

So audacious a policy and one so regardless of religious affiliations provoked bitter controversy both within France and outside it, and if in the reign of Francis I the Turkish alliance was the object of violent criticism, in the time of Richelieu the Protestant alliances unleashed storms of protest. There is no need to set forth in detail the arguments which were adduced to justify them. We need note only the principal preoccupation of the apologists which was to draw a precise distinction between political interests and purely religious interests. The first-named were pointed out to be secular in character, being founded on international law and on the natural solidarity existing between men. Ecclesiastical law, on which the last-named depend, was shown not to have suppressed the common law of humanity. In an apologetic memorandum which Francis I addressed to the Pope in 1543, this distinction is already clearly drawn. Jean du Bellay defends himself against

the objections of opponents, based on St. Paul's words:—
"What harmony between Christ and Belial? How can a
believer throw in his lot with an infidel?" (II Cor. vi. 15).
The general trend of his defence is that, whilst there exists
between Christians and Turks a profound difference both in
habits and in religion, this difference affects only the moral
code, it does not destroy the participation of both peoples in a
single human nature. It is this common nature which forms the
basis of alliances between nations.[4]

In the time of Richelieu we find a similar affirmation in
favour of the right to carry out a secular policy, independent in
so far as the Church was concerned, but dependent on the *Jus
Gentium* and the moral law. On the pretext of religion, remarks
an adherent of the cardinal, the right is claimed to release
Catholic subjects from allegiance to a Protestant State; but, he
replies, quoting St. Thomas, "whilst the divine law draws a
distinction between believers and infidels, it nevertheless does
not abrogate the human law, founded on nature, according to
which infidels may bear rule over believers"; therefore, in
order to preserve one's rights, one is entitled to form alliances
with the former.[5] In less guarded fashion, another controversialist wrote:—"It does not matter at all whether those with
whom one enters into a confederation are Catholics or not,
since the matter is merely one of human rights."[6] A friend of
Richelieu, the Bishop of Chartres, summed up the matter
concisely by stressing at once the agreement reached between
the two powers and their respective independence:—"Religion
and the dignity of the State give each other mutual support and,
by means of a reasonable agreement, learn to live in sweet
harmony. Nevertheless, both have their separate rights and
each is confined within its proper limits; for it is not permitted
to the State to violate religion or to religion to overthrow the
State."[7]

*     *     *

It was once again with a view to resisting the Spanish
hegemony that the French monarchy made use of arguments
of a purely secular kind to defend its own rights of colonization.
In 1493, when Christopher Columbus first returned from

America, Pope Alexander VI undertook to mediate between Spain and Portugal in the matter of their claims upon the New World. The Bull *Inter cætera*, modified in the following year by the Treaty of Tordesillas, divided into two zones the territories to which both aspired. The meridian which runs 370 leagues west of the Azores was chosen by the Pope as the line of demarcation. All the territory to the west of this line was to revert to Spain; all that to the east of it was to fall beneath the sway of Portugal. It was for this reason that Brazil, when discovered, came under the rule of the Portuguese monarchy. Long discussions ensured later as to the exact sense and scope of this Bull, their Catholic Majesties hastening to interpret it, as their temporal interests dictated, in the most rigorous sense: "the Pope is Suzerain of the world, he bestows the territories of the infidels on whom he will".

When the French made their first attempts to found colonies in Brazil, in Canada and in Florida, the Spanish Court of course appealed to the Papal Bull to justify their claim to sovereign rights over these territories. But His Most Christian Majesty, far from giving way, boldly resisted all such extravagant pretensions. Here again, it is interesting to note, the attitude adopted by France in opposition to Spain assumed an anti-clerical character. The latter, as we have seen, rested its claim entirely on ecclesiastical law. France, regarding the partition decreed by Alexander VI as null and void, appealed in this quarrel solely to the maxims of natural law: free trade and navigation of the seas, legal right of the first occupant. From the time of Francis I onwards, a whole series of protests served to recall to the Peninsular powers these accepted principles of the *Jus Gentium*. On no occasion did the two points of view clash more sharply than at the Conversations of Cateau-Cambrésis in 1559:

> We have struggled hard [the representatives of Spain wrote to their master] to exclude the French from navigating to the Indies, but we have not been able to persuade them to exclude their subjects from such navigation; they made use of the ordinary arguments about the freedom of the seas . . . We, on the other hand, based ourselves on the Bulls of Pope Alexander and of Julius II, and on the message which was

sent to the Christian princes to find out whether these would contribute to the expenses of the discovery and of the demarcation of territory which followed it.[8]

We do not conclude from the above that the French Crown imposed upon its colonies a secularist policy. The conversion of the natives was in fact a constant source of solicitude to the Royal Government—both in the Antilles and in Canada. It is, however, true that, unlike Catholic Spain, the eldest daughter of the Church had every intention of freeing her colonial enterprises from all control by the Holy See.

\*         \*         \*

After colonial policy, internal policy was in its turn influenced by secularist tendencies. Up to the end of the reign of Henry II, the unity of Faith throughout the kingdom was insisted upon rigorously. The Chancellor Michel de l'Hospital, affirmed this principle, as late as December, 1560, before the deputies of the States General: "The division of tongues does not cause the separation of kingdoms, but that of religion and laws which out of one kingdom makes two.   Hence the old maxim: 'One faith, one law, one king'."[9] The adherents of the Reformation in its early days were made to feel the full rigour of this principle. As enemies of the Faith, they at one and the same time threatened the internal unity of the kingdom and laid themselves open to terrible penalties. In the countries where the new religion triumphed, it had no hesitation in displaying the same spirit of intolerance to its own advantage. Henry VIII in England, Calvin in Geneva, bore witness to this by their deeds. In Germany the Peace of Augsburg (1555), despite appearances, was really far from being a liberal solution. For although it undoubtedly recognized the right of Lutheran and Catholic principalities to peaceful co-existence, it gave each Prince the power of enforcing his own religion in his own territory. Dissident subjects, in fact, found themselves faced by this cruel alternative: either to become converted to the official religion, or to quit the country.

France, unlike the Empire, was not a mosaic of sovereign States. Louis XI and Francis I between them had made it into a united nation, strongly centralized; and the formation of a solid Protestant minority—dating from the time of Charles IX —had since then led to the acceptance of novel political solutions. After more than thirty years of civil war, with all its alarming fluctuations, the State at least came to distinguish, to some extent, between the idea of political unity in France and that of religious unity.

The party known as *Les Politiques* have often been praised for having recognized at so early a date the solutions of the future: a tolerant policy and the secularization of the State. In reality, however, their attitude was less clear-cut than this; and it is a significant fact that their spokesman in the States General of 1560 by no means repudiated the traditional maxim: "One faith, one law, one king." Besides it was for a long time believed in France that a Council would eventually succeed in putting things to rights and in re-establishing religious unity throughout the kingdom. Thus the first solution proposed by *Les Politiques* was no more than a provisional tolerance with a view to facilitating the return of the Protestants to Catholic unity. Thus it was that, at the States General of 1560, the Abbé de Bois-Aubry said:— "Pending this Council, it is necessary that we should live in peace, practising one or other of the two religions."[10] In the following year Michel de l'Hospital proposed, in similar fashion, to the States General that they should await the fuller solution which reflexion might bring, not stiffening their attitude towards the evangelicals but merely taking precautions lest any sedition should make itself felt.[11] Fifteen years later, the Duc d'Alençon, who had by then assumed the leadership of *Les Politiques*, once again expressed the hope that "the religious question might be solved by means of a sacred Council".[12]

The original intention of only granting provisional tolerance is easily understandable. According to the universal conviction of those days, any diversity of religion in a State was bound to lead in the end to disorder and sedition. "It is folly," said the Chancellor to the States General in 1560, "to hope for peace, tranquillity or friendship between people of different religions. There is indeed no kind of opinion which sinks so deeply into the heart of man as religious opinion, or any which cuts men off so completely from one another".[13]

In the light of experience it was appreciated, however, that the attempt to restore religious unity at any cost might mean endangering the very foundations of the State and, since the Protestant schism proved to be lasting and the conciliary solution illusory, the principle of civil toleration ended by gaining ground. So far back as 1561 we find the anonymous author of the *Exhortation aux Princes* admitting that, whilst it is possible to suppress a new sect in its infancy, it is "fatal for a country to attempt to do so when it is already full-grown". Utterly sceptical as to the possibility of a Council's coping with the situation, the same author proposed to the Queen that "the existence of two Churches in the Realm should be allowed". This solution seemed to him all the more urgent in view of the fact that "the stranger at our gates", by which he meant Spain, was always on the alert, ready to "profit by our internal discords in order to meddle more and more closely in the affairs of France".[14] After the failure of the Poissy conversations, even Michel de l'Hospital lost much of his original optimism as regards councils and conferences. The chief object of the old Chancellor's exhortations was henceforth the *political* reconciliation of Protestants and Catholics, of which he suggested that the basis should be the loyalty of both parties alike to the person of the Sovereign. "It is quite certain", he wrote in 1570 in an appeal to Charles IX, "that amongst all those who to-day have taken up arms . . . there is none who does not recognize in him (Charles) his rightful King, and his Sovereign and sole Prince". The King's duty is, therefore, he says, to act as a good father of the family and to reconcile his warring sons, since "in that direction lies the security of the Realm".[15]

It thus appeared to *Les Politiques* that the exigencies of national unity and those of religious unity were not to be placed on the same plane: if the State should try to identify them at all costs, it would be jeopardizing its own existence. "It may be", wrote Jean Bodin in *La République* (1576), "that the sectarian community is so powerful that it is impossible to destroy it. In cases of that kind princes of the wiser type have been in the habit of behaving like those prudent pilots who allow themselves to be driven by the storm, well knowing that to put up any resistance is to court complete shipwreck".[16]

In the year 1576, *Les Politiques* obtained a noteworthy concession, when the Protestants were granted, in the Edict of Beaulieu, full liberty of worship in all the towns and villages of France, Paris alone excepted. In face, however, of the sharp reaction of intransigent Catholics, this concession was short-lived and, already reduced in scope by the Edict of Poitiers (1557), it was lost sight of for a long period amidst the disorders engendered by the League and by the anarchic state of France.

This premature victory was not, however, fruitless. Twenty years later, what Père de la Brière has described as "a social necessity stronger than the will of men" resulted in the re-entry into force of the forgotten edicts. Less liberal in character than the Edict of Beaulieu, the Edict of Nantes (1598) restricted the places of worship of the reformed religion to two places in each bailiwick, to 3,500 castles, and to the towns actually held by the Protestants on the 31st August, 1597. Essentially practical in character, this celebrated document did not give expression to any general principle in regard to relations between the State and the dissident sects. It was simply an act of pacification. It did not however contain any allusion, as previous documents, including the Edict of Poitiers, had done, to the "free and lawful General Council". It thus lacked the character of a provisional transaction which previous edicts had possessed. Henceforth, even though the Catholic Faith remained the sole State religion, adhesion to the official Church was no longer regarded as a *sine qua non* of political loyalty. Fidelity to the person of the Sovereign no longer necessarily involved communion with him in the same external religion. Here we have in fact a new secularization of the State, a situation to which substantial expression was given by Henry IV in his address to the *Parlement* of Paris, some days before the promulgation of the Edict. "No distinction", he said, "must henceforth be made between Catholics and Huguenots, but all must be good Frenchmen, and let the Catholics endeavour to convert the Huguenots by the example of a good life".[17]

After having been faithfully observed by Henry IV, the Edict of Nantes was maintained under Louis XIII (in spite of the opposition of intransigent Catholics) by the courageous action of Richelieu. This great Minister of State applied in detail the principles which he had formulated, as far back as 1616, in his instructions to Schomberg. "Different beliefs", he had then said, "do not make us into different States; separated in faith, we remain united in one prince, in whose service no Catholic is so blind as to regard—where matters of State are concerned— a Spaniard as better than a French Huguenot."[18] He definitely crushed the Reformers as a political party, but he consistently opposed the use of violence against individuals and religious communities as such.

*     *     *

In the triple domain of foreign alliances, of colonial affairs and of internal government, the French monarchy in the modern epoch certainly displayed considerable courage. In several matters of policy it resolutely disassociated profane from religious interests, and reproaches were often levelled against it on this account. Indeed, from both inside and outside the kingdom complaints continued to be raised against so novel an attitude, and one so much at variance with medieval tradition. Even in our own day, certain foreign historians, voicing afresh, after three centuries, the grievances of the *parti dévot*, go so far as to bring the gravest accusations against—for example— Richelieu. An English Catholic, Mr. Hilaire Belloc,[19] represents the great Minister of Louis XIII as the grave-digger of traditional Christianity; he even reproaches him with having, by his internal policy, perpetuated religious divisions in France. This severe judgment seems to us to lack justification. Later on, we shall criticize certain of the maxims which inspired the Cardinal's rule; but surely it is unjust to accuse him of having ruined forever the Christian unity of Europe? That had already crumbled beneath the hammer-blows of the Reformation, its restoration by the House of Austria had been no more than a caricature of what had been, the deceptive cloak for temporal hegemony on a huge scale. As regards the religious division of France, thirty years of civil war had proved it to be irremediable; it is to Richelieu's credit that he did not try, once again, to impose a solution by force; he was acting consistently when he tried to strengthen national unity without again risking its submergence in the whirlpool of religious strife.

That such a policy should have given rise in its time to passionate controversy we are not concerned to deny; but it was not the cause of universal scandal to pious souls which some imagine. A sufficient proof of this can be found in the very wise comments of an eminent Jesuit, Père Lallemant, who died in 1635 and who was and remains one of the great spiritual masters of the Society of Jesus.[20]

> It is common [he wrote] for men to speak very thoughtlessly about affairs of State. We ought not to speak either favourably or unfavourably about matters of this kind without having received supernatural enlightenment. It is possible to make two mistakes in this direction, one being to approve and praise certain things on mere impulse, the other to condemn and blame them with rash haste. Thus, for instance, when Catholic princes form alliances with heretics, men either favour unduly the cause of these allied heretics, and speak too enthusiastically of their success, which gives rise to many scruples and sins; or else, they express disapproval of some of their rulers' actions in favour of these same allies, thereby showing a misguided zeal and a failure to understand that God can cause these actions to produce many good results which are hidden from us. We must not by any means censure such actions by princes or ministers, but must let God act, awaiting with patience, and in silence, the outcome of events which Providence will cause to meet with success and to redound to His glory.

After three centuries, an historian is surely justified in showing no greater severity towards the French monarchy than did Père Lallemant. The partial secularization of its policy was forced upon it by events, nor was it for reasons of vulgar ambition that the Most Christian Kings called upon Turks or Protestant powers for assistance. It was the foreign menace which forced this course upon them, in spite of their personal reluctance and the protests of public opinion. Thus it was not out of defiance to the Holy See that they granted certain religious liberties to the Protestant party, it was because, after a long series of civil wars, this appeared to be the only acceptable solution. Nor was it in a rebellious spirit that they denied all temporal validity to the Bull of Alexander VI; all that they were doing was to register their protest against an indefensible interpretation of the Bull of which the Spanish rivals of France were making use to their own great advantage.

Besides, these measures, though unprecedented, did not go beyond the normal limits of State independence. Based on the exigencies of national life, they affirmed the right of States, when it was a question of safeguarding their material existence, to show a relative independence in respect of religious and confessional divisions. "The State not having religion for its end", writes a modern theologian, "does not see in religion the principle of its unity . . . It is thus untrue to say that religious unity is what causes the unity of the State . . . Present-day States, in which this unity is lacking, are thus not essentially vitiated."[21] These reflexions by Père Vermeersch would have given scandal at the beginning of the sixteenth century. The difference in order and in nature between Church and State, though clearly marked out by Thomist theologians, still remained in the realm of academic theory. Cases of conscience, such as those arising from the Reformation and from Spanish imperialism, had to present themselves before these principles could be applied in the concrete; and the interesting thing about French policy at this period is that it did throw into high relief a problem which still faces us, that of the necessity and of the limits of State secularization.

The political measures which caused so much of a sensation amongst the contemporaries of Richelieu were little by little accepted as reasonable. Not without setbacks, it is true, since, under Louis XIV, the Revocation of the Edict of Nantes destroyed at one blow the work of reconciliation carried out by his predecessors. Gradually, however, the difficulties were surmounted and in our day States are not concerned with differences of religion when they form alliances; they no longer have recourse to Papal Bulls in order to justify their colonial ambitions; they grant to all sects, within the limits compatible with public order, the benefits of civil tolerance. All these acts which give practical expression to the lay and profane character of the State appear as lawful *per se* in the eyes of Catholic theology. The latter does however impose two essential conditions: every secular government is bound to respect in its administration the rules of the moral law and of the *Jus Gentium*; and it must work in harmony with the Church with a view to ensuring that the realization of its temporal aims does not raise obstacles to the spiritual ends of man. Now it is precisely this twofold claim on the part of the Church which the modern lay State refuses to admit.

## 2.  MODERN REGALISM

The secularization of French politics in the modern epoch has so far appeared to us as the inevitable consequence of the religious revolution and of the break-up of the old Christian order. The idea was, however, destined to be extended, and in a highly dangerous manner, as a result of the popularization of audacious theories in regard to the power and government of the State. It is possible to date from the Renaissance the efflorescence of these new tendencies in political life. The Renaissance did not in fact tend only towards the liberation and exaltation of the individual; it also did much to free from all moral and religious restraint the person of the Prince and the sovereignty of the State. It thus transformed into unbridled laicism the movement of State secularization to which the Church was able, by and large, to accommodate herself. We may reduce the movement to two main essentials: the diffusion of Machiavellian methods of government, and a tenderness for the new absolutist conceptions of the State and of sovereignty.

\*          \*          \*

This is no place to set out in detail the system of Machiavelli, but we would point out, with the best commentators on his work, that its most striking characteristic is the complete absence from it of any moral standards. His political theory is merely the technique of success, carried out regardless of the justice or injustice of the means employed. It is as independent of the moral law as it is of the prescriptions of the Church.

Such is indeed admitted by friends and foes alike to be the salient characteristic of the Machiavellian system. If it is desired to form an opinion of the influence which it has exerted, it is not enough to take into consideration the few works that have been avowedly written in its defence or the impressively numerous refutations. This, we think, would lead the student to conclude incorrectly that these views had obtained no great hold, whilst actually Machiavellianism is taught, even though in small doses, in a large number of political works. Even those authors who set out to refute it are rarely uninfected themselves, and M. Charles Benoist thought fit to entitle one of his books: *Le Machiavelisme de l'Anti-Machiavel*. Statesmen draw inspiration from Machiavelli's ideas and act upon his advice. The expression most typical of the whole system, that is, "political expediency" or *raison d'état*, has become a favourite phrase in modern times. It is true that the expression is not itself found in Machiavelli's works but it sums up his teaching. It appeared in Italy towards the middle of the sixteenth century, and soon enjoyed a popularity which quickly increased.[22] It is generally associated with the idea of a "realist" policy exclusively concerned with the interests of the State in their crudest and most egoistic form.

In his *Testament politique* Richelieu denied that he had fallen into this error and positively recommended, for instance, that treaties should be conscientiously observed. He did however admit frankly that many politicians taught otherwise and it may be asked whether he did not himself, in certain of his "State Maxims", place too wide a gulf between State morals and private morals.

> Affairs of State [he there wrote] are not like other affairs. In the one case, we have to begin by elucidation of rights, in the other by execution and possession. In the course of ordinary affairs, justice demands clear evidence and proofs . . . But it is not the same with affairs of State, where it is a matter of the *summa rerum*. For often conjectures have to take the place of proofs, seeing that great designs and important enterprises are never achieved otherwise than by the success or fulfilment of the same, whence there can be no appeal.[23]

In a still less discreet manner, certain defenders of the cardinal and his policy explained, as best they could, the principles of political expediency: "The laws of the State are different to those of the casuists", declared Jérémie Ferrier, "and the maxims of the Schools have nothing to do with politics . . . The wars of great kings are not subject to the laws of theologians, and amidst the armies Justice speaks in an undertone . . ."[24] Eustache de Refuge recognized that for reasons of State security, the Prince may find himself "obliged to step aside from the ordinary way of justice"; he should doubtless do so with regret, but with a resolution as firm as that of a father who cauterizes or cuts off the limb of his child in order to save his life.[25] Balzac in *Aristippe* was only reflecting certain opinions then current when he addressed to Louis XIII the following remarkable pieces of advice:[26]

> The world lost its innocence long ago. We are far gone in the corruption of the ages and in the decay of nature . . . If you wish to work successfully for the good of the State, adapt yourself to the defects and imperfections of your material. Rid yourself of that inconvenient virtue which has no place in the age in which you live. There are maxims which are not just by nature but which usage justifies. There are filthy remedies which are none the less remedies. These salutary remedies involve human blood, excrement and other foul things, but the beauty of health compensates for this foulness. There are cases in which poison heals, and then poison is no longer evil.

The epoch of Richelieu even saw the publication of regular apologies for Machiavelli and his doctrine. That written by Claude Machon, canon of Toul, remained in manuscript form, but was drawn up with the cardinal's approval and completed soon after his death, in 1643. It may be noted that, like Balzac's *Aristippe*, it makes use of the theme of the corruption of the world and of the general triumph of vice over virtue:

> That is why Machiavelli, seeing virtue to be so ineffective and ill rewarded, made his Prince adapt himself to the humours of men and, unwilling that an angel should be abandoned amongst brutes, *separated the interests of conscience from those of the State* and, only considering the best means of preserving temporal goods, gave advice and counsel which he thought to be infallible and necessary for the good governance of his kingdom and its maintenance among men.[27]

In his book *Considérations politiques sur les Coups d'Etat*, which appeared in 1639, during the lifetime of Richelieu, Gabriel Naudé, Mazarin's learned librarian, drew a distinction between *Maximes d'Etat* and *Coups d'Etat*. The first, he said, corresponded to the *Ragion di Stato* of the Italians; they signified those acts by government which civil law and the *Jus Gentium* disallowed, but which considerations of public welfare and discipline made permissible. *Coups d'Etat* were distinguished from these by their violent and sudden character. St. Bartholomew's Eve provided the most famous example; and Naudé remarked that, if it had received so much blame, this was in his opinion primarily due to the fact that "the business was only half completed". After having quoted other similar measures, the author concluded, not without irony: "These examples will also serve as very genuine proofs that, although Machiavelli's writings are forbidden, his doctrine has not ceased to be practised, even by those who authorized its being censured and prohibited".28

Machiavellianism involves in practice the excessive laicizing of civil government. It is a form of utilitarianism which is cunning or brutal, according to circumstances, and which pays little heed, in moments of embarrassment, to moral and religious requirements. It must not of course be confused with tact or prudence in the art of government. If it sometimes gives the impression or bears the outward appearance of being no more than this, it essentially differs from it in the motives which inspire its action. Prudence involves remaining faithful to the ideal of justice, even though it may be ready to reach that end somewhat circuitously. Machiavellianism, on the other hand, is a policy which subordinates everything to success, which it seeks to obtain by all possible means, being perfectly ready the while to sweep aside any inconvenient moral considerations, or precepts of international law. The lengths to which it can be pushed of course vary greatly in degree, and our barbarous epoch may consider that its manifestations in former ages were very half-hearted. Once the principles of Machiavellianism have been accepted, it is however difficult to draw the line and the danger of unbridled excess is greatly increased when the atmosphere is materialistic and irreligious. All serious resistance then vanishes and, as the cruel experiences of our own day have shown, the doctrine of political expediency assumes alike the most immoral and the most oppressive forms.

★     ★     ★

Machiavellianism, being essentially opportunist, has no prejudices in regard either to the nature or the basis of the State and can make itself felt in any régime and under all forms of government. There exists, however, a form of lay State which causes us even graver and deeper anxiety, since its acceptance undermines the very source of political authority: we refer to the *absolutist* conception of the State and of authority.

It was in 1576 that the first modern work on the notion of sovereignty, the *République* of Jean Bodin, appeared in print. The author revived the Roman theory of the *imperium* and defined it briefly as "the absolute and *perpetual power of a realm*".[29] We note at once the highly abstract character of this definition. Sovereignty is pictured as hovering over various régimes in any one of which it may become incarnate. Whether it be a monarchy, or an aristocratic or democratic State that is in question, it preserves its character and attributes. The forms of government may vary, the sovereignty remains immutable. It is *perpetual*, and princes exercise it for life in accordance with the rules governing their succession, while democratic States likewise possess it in virtue of the continuity of their political forms. It is *absolute*, for the authority which it confers is super-eminent and demands from subjects an obedience subject to no reserves. From this last attribute springs the *indivisibility* of the sovereign power: if two princes, Bodin tells us, are equal within one realm, "neither the one nor the other is sovereign, but it may properly be said that both together hold sovereignty over the State".[30]

It is usually said that the beginning of the modern epoch coincides—in France and in Europe generally—with the advent of absolutism, and by this last term is meant kingship by Divine Right which identifies itself with the State, according to the celebrated formula:—"*L'Etat, c'est moi.*" Before proceeding any further we should however do well to note that, before becoming in any way associated with the person of the King, the absolutist idea had deeply penetrated the whole concept of the State and the whole idea of sovereignty. Here was a revolution destined to have a far more important effect upon the future than any temporary phenomenon such as that of absolute monarchy.

"Absolutism", wrote M. Déclareuil in his *Histoire générale du Droit français*:[31]

consists in identifying with the State, considered as an entity, the whole national existence. There is nothing which does not emanate from the State or at least which can exist without the State's permission; it alone creates and founds; nothing can continue to exist unless it retains the favour of the State; having created, it can destroy. The State absorbs or holds in check all the activities of other bodies, both setting them in motion and reaping the benefits that accrue therefrom. Since absolutism is identical with the omnipotence of the State and excludes the existence of independent institutions outside it, the constitutional form of the State matters but little.

The forms of the State can change: the monarchy of the *ancien régime* is not the same as the Jacobin Republic, and the latter is not the same as the Empire. Again, the State can become incarnate in a single person, or in several associated organs which only possess sovereignty when combined into one whole. The power of the State, however, remains untouched, and remains—according to these modern ideas—absolute.

The essentially secularist and lay character of this conception of the State will at once be noted. As being an abstract political power, sovereignty does not, as such, bear any relationship to religious doctrine. It is independent of the Church and of Revelation, nor is it tied to any theory of the Divine Right of Kings. It cannot therefore render itself liable to criticism on either of those scores. As we have seen, the view that the State is of purely secular and natural origin does not present any difficulty from the point of view of Catholic doctrine. No, if modern theories about the State have proved to be dangerous and liable to abuse, it is because they emphasize, with growing insistence, the exclusive character of this secular sovereignty. By this means they have laid the foundations of a lay absolutism which, far from vanishing with the *ancien régime*, has grown more

exacting and more tyrannical. They have laicized the old
conception of Caesaro-papism, thereby rendering it more
repellent than ever to religious-minded people, since, under
its new form of "modern regalism", it has lost all sense of
a spiritual mission whilst continuing to exercise over the Church
and ecclesiastical discipline an absolute right of domination.

The danger was already serious enough during the last
centuries of the old monarchy. After Jean Bodin, the defenders
of the Absolute Power laid stress, in their arguments, on the
indivisible character of sovereignty. "It is no more divisible,"
said Le Bret, "than a point in geometry."[32] "It is a contradictory proposition," we read in an anonymous treatise on the
Royal Authority (1691), "that there can be in a single State
two distinct sovereign powers, equal or subordinate, which
reside in distinct subjects."[33]

We can see at once to what difficulties this principle can
give rise in the matter of the exercise of ecclesiastical jurisdiction.
How, for instance, will it enable us to reconcile the King's
sovereignty with the Pope's authority over the clergy in the
kingdom? Will not this imply a division of sovereignty incompatible with the fashionable theory of State authority?
Thus it was that the defenders of absolutism always regarded
with a mistrustful eye the Holy See and its claims to universal jurisdiction. Political Gallicanism, although it no doubt
existed before the sixteenth century, underwent a dangerous
development at that period, owing to the new conceptions
regarding the attributes of sovereignty. In the eyes of the
Gallican *parlementaires*, all jurisdiction of whatever kind derived
from the State and was under its control. There was no need
in this connexion to appeal to the rights of the King or to
the sacred character of his person. He possessed full control
over the Church because he was the incarnation of sovereignty.
"As ecclesiastical jurisdiction", wrote Lebret, "was established
by the authority of sovereign princes, it follows that whenever
it has attempted to go beyond its appointed limits, it has again
become subject to their sovereign power."[34]

In practice, according to the secularist theorists of *Les
Libertés de l'Eglise Gallicane*—those "liberties" which Fénelon
described with such truth as "servitudes"—the Pope could

only exercise his spiritual power in France under the strict control of the State authorities. All kinds of obstacles came to be placed in the way of his exercise of jurisdiction in the realm of France. Legates, Papal Bulls, the relations of bishops and Religious Orders with the Holy See, all were affected; indeed no subject of the King was allowed to have direct recourse to the Court of Rome in order to put his spiritual affairs in order. The more extreme Gallicans compared the Papacy to a foreign power to the meddling of which a halt must be called:

> Our liberties [wrote d'Agnesseau in 1703] do not merely prevent us from accepting laws which are contrary to our customs, but also from having any laws other than our own on matters which regard questions of public order and discipline. Any action initiated by a foreign power within this realm must always be suspect even though it appears to be entirely innocent; thus, the Papal Brief (on the Jansenist controversy) may be, if you will, a just ordinance, necessary and conducive to peace in the Church; but it is at the same time the work of a foreign power which has no immediate authority amongst us in any matters which have to do with public order and discipline. This is a sufficient reason for declining to accept it.[35]

Now there is no spiritual end which can be held to justify measures which thus restrict the papal authority. In fact they have only one end and that essentially material: namely to maintain the absolute and indivisible character of secular sovereignty.

Generally speaking, this new political dogma would seem to push to extremes the doctrine of State Expediency. Everything in national life, including religion, must—it is averred—be ordered and administered with exclusive regard to the interests of the temporal sovereignty. This political secularism was, in monarchical France, kept in check by the Christian sentiments of the French Kings, their anxiety not to break with the Holy See, and the attachment to the Church which the whole nation shared. None the less, it implied a grave threat to the spiritual society, for if religion really derives to this extent from the temporal power, it may be treated by the State as it chooses, according to the fluctuating interests of the

latter. Thus, a favourable attitude may be succeeded by one
of indifference, and hard upon indifference may tread hostility.
The absolute sovereignty of the State logically allows of all
these attitudes.

*          *          *

In order to recognize in its various aspects the same phenomenon of absolutism, one would need to study carefully the
history of recent centuries; but a few chosen examples will
suffice for our purpose. As we have just seen, modern regalism
made its appearance in France under the form of parliamentary
Gallicanism, but—as was to be expected—by no means
neglected to make itself felt in the countries won by the
Reformation. Under the influence of the new doctrines, the
Caesaro-papism with which the movement had started was
gradually replaced by a secularized version of the theory.
In the eyes of the German Reformers, the primary obligation
of the Prince was to perform spiritual functions; was he not
the shepherd, the bishop, of his subjects? A theory entitled
"Episcopalism", which was elaborated towards the end of the
sixteenth century furnished a juridical basis for the dual power
of the temporal sovereign, but such pretty fancies bore but
little relation to the grim reality. The "episcopal" power as
exercised by the Prince was nothing but a new instrument of
tyranny. More in accordance with the facts and the new doctrines was a different juridical system devised by Grotius and
the German school of Natural Law; this was known as
"Territorialism"[36] and took the view that the State had special
powers—constituting the *jus circa sacra*—over the Churches and
over divine worship; this was an integral part of its territorial
rights corresponding to the rights which it possessed over the
police, the army or finance. What it actually amounted to was
an absolute and indivisible sovereignty which the Prince
incarnated in his own person.

An evolution of the same type took place in Protestant
England. The quasi-pontifical power which Henry VIII
originally claimed for himself soon became—first in act and
later in theory—a simple attribute of the royal prerogative.
In the eyes of Francis Bacon, John Selden and Thomas Hobbes,

there is no independent ecclesiastical jurisdiction: all jurisdiction derives from the King and from his temporal supremacy.

Thus possessed of an entirely secular and yet unlimited sovereignty, Protestant kings and princes proceeded to treat religion in whatever way the exigencies of their policy demanded. In the early days they thought it more practical to insist upon religious unity within their frontiers—*cujus regio, ejus religio*—and anyone who did not belong to the Prince's religion must emigrate to another State. This Clause of the Peace of Augsburg (1555), modified only in certain particulars, appeared once more in the Peace of Westphalia (1648). It was the same in England where the Stuart monarchy only recognized one Church and persecuted all dissidents. The action of Louis XIV, when he repealed the Edict of Nantes in 1685, was a manifestation of a similar policy. The devout folk of the time imagined this measure to have been inspired by religious conviction but in fact it was due much less to the King's zeal for the Church than to his urge towards absolutism. Anxious as he was to assert his authority over religion, as over everything else, Louis XIV thought that the simplest thing would be to unify it—*cujus regio, ejus religio*.

In the light of experience, however, the maintenance of a single religion began to appear more onerous than profitable to the exponents of modern regalism. Without in any way loosening their hold upon the official Church, they found it advisable to grant the benefits of tolerance to certain dissident Churches. This practice took its rise in the seventeenth century in certain German principalities such as Brandenburg, and in England after the Revolution of 1688. Afterwards it became one of the characteristic features of the system of "enlightened despotism". After Frederick the Great of Prussia, the most typical exponent of this theory was a Catholic sovereign, the Emperor Joseph II of Austria. Convinced, like the Gallicans, that all authority derives from the secular sovereignty, this "royal sacristan" meddled with all the Church's concerns and, even against the Pope's will, took active steps to reform abuses, whilst at the same time, by the Edict of Tolerance of 1781, he granted civil equality and the free exercise of their religion to Protestants. It is easy to note from this instance the distinction between the Catholic doctrine of tolerance and the conceptions of "enlightened despotism". The latter, like all types of regalism, continued to affirm its right to control the Churches; it granted them religious liberty only in the name of its temporal interests. A Catholic Minister like Richelieu, on the other hand, was ready to grant civil tolerance to Protestants because he refused to put the affairs of the State and those of religion on the same plane.

The French Revolution took over at one and the same time the Gallican traditions and the heritage of enlightened despotism. As absolute in its own way as ever the philosopher-kings had been, it proclaimed liberty of worship and simultaneously forced upon the Gallican Church a statute which both detached that body from Rome and enslaved it to the State. We know what followed and what tragic consequences the Civil Constitution of the Clergy brought in its train: the schism which rent France, the persecution of the refractory clergy, the massacres and the Reign of Terror. From that time forward, secular absolutism displayed its full virulence. In the time of Louis XIV, it had thought fit to favour the Church and repress the Protestants; a century later, still consulting its own exclusive interests, it proceeded, as and when it chose, to persecute the Catholic Church, to emancipate the Reformed sects and to institute—on various occasions—entirely new forms of worship.

It was this same secular regalism which served to ruin the Church's relations with the temporal power in the nineteenth century. It is a curious fact that, whilst governments laicized themselves and ministers prided themselves on their rationalist views, they none the less continued to meddle with jealous obstinacy in the affairs and in the discipline of the Church; and the reason for this must be sought in the survival in these men of the spirit of Gallicanism and also of Josephism. No authority, it seemed to them, not even that of religion, could be exercised except with the approval, and under the control, of the State. The Concordat of 1801, for example, in spite of all the advantages which it gave to the French Government, was incapable of satisfying their thirst for domination and the Imperial Government appended to it, under the name of

*Articles organiques*, the most characteristic of the old Gallican maxims. The modern reader is indeed surprised by the strange intrusions into the spiritual field which he here discovers . . . How can a "lay" power suppose itself to have the right to force upon the clergy a unified liturgy and catechism; upon bishops, the canonical obligation to reside in their sees; upon professors of seminaries, the four articles of 1682? How can the secular authority be acquitted of meddling in Church affairs when it renders dependent on its own *placet* the acts of the *magisterium* or of the spiritual authority: Papal Bulls, actions of Papal legates, appeals by the bishops to Rome to give an account of their ministry? . . . And yet this imperial regulation was to remain in force for a whole century, and even the Third Republic was to sponsor it until a day came when a sectarian majority denounced the Concordat and, under the pretext of "separatism", subjected the French clergy to a new type of enslavement and persecution. It must be remembered indeed that, whilst the word "separatism" is susceptible of a liberal interpretation, it is also used to cover a form of despotism in regard to which Emile Ollivier justly stated that "beneath the appearances of liberty we here have concealed one of the completest forms of that regalism whereby the State is enabled to oppress the Church".[37] Separatism in fact consists in reducing the Church from the rank of a public institution to that of a private society and, once that has been done, we can see how easy it is for a persecuting government, if it so desires, to apply to her not the common law but emergency legislation of the most damaging kind.

A glance through the history of the absolutist experiment is enough to leave it self-condemned. The enslavement of the spiritual society to a secular power must lead, in the last analysis, to one of two things: the decadence of religion, or the persecution of both flock and shepherd. Not only the facts, but religious sentiment as well, condemn all such developments. Nothing indeed can be more intolerable to the true believer than to see his Church placed at the mercy of a secular, a Voltairean or an anti-religious government. We may recall in this connexion the bitter comment of Lamennais during the first press campaign conducted by the *Avenir* in October, 1830.[38]

Consider the inevitable consequences of the enslavement (of the Church); work out, if you can, the future results of any prolongation of a state of affairs which has already proved so disastrous: religion administered like the customs or excise, the priesthood degraded, discipline ruined, education obstructed, the Church, in a word, deprived of her essential independence, daily finding it more difficult to communicate with her Head and daily more harshly subjected to the whims of the temporal power, made in every respect the mere plaything of the State, receiving everything from it, pastors, laws, even doctrine. What can that be called but death?

A great deal of fuss has been made about clericalism since the beginning of the Third Republic. We have taken this grievance into account and have not withheld such criticism as was due. This does not mean, however, that we are in the least prepared to condone one of the principal scandals of recent centuries: the establishment of control over religion and public worship by hostile or irreligious governments: the interference in spiritual affairs of a power which makes a mere mock of religion. Such excesses enable us to appreciate better, by force of contrast, the extreme wisdom of the Catholic doctrine. The question of Church and State is not a question of domination. It does not involve our enquiring which of the two powers is to subjugate the other and enforce its laws upon it. It is above all a question of harmony and of balance. It can only be resolved by means of a friendly understanding between the two powers, each of them deeply engrossed in its own distinct mission but each working definitely for the common good of mankind.

### 3. LIBERAL SEPARATISM

The lay State can make itself manifest either in totalitarian or in liberal guise. In its first form it subjects the Church to strict control and dominates her in every way; in its second form, it affects to ignore the Church in order to confine itself to its temporal ends, it refuses to recognize the Church as anything more than an ordinary association free to benefit by the provisions of common law.

Liberal secularism, as we have already seen, cannot consistently be reconciled with all forms of separatism, for to subject religious societies to Draconian laws, of a kind which undermine their basic statutes, is certainly not the same as ignoring the Church: it is tantamount to an attempt to destroy or at least to oppress her. We must therefore set aside as evidently anti-liberal certain historical exemplifications of the separatist idea. Amongst these may be mentioned the first French Law of Separation (21st February, 1795). The views of the contrivers of this law are to be found, expressed with great frankness, in the report of Boissy d'Anglas. His comments may be summed up as follows. "Persecution is powerless against the Church; we have at our disposal, however, a surer means of attaining our end, namely that of reducing Catholicism to the status of a miserable sect, provided with a minimum of liberty. No more State religion, no more budget for public worship; let everything that could confer any prestige upon religion be removed from it; let its services be allowed to take place in private houses only, let all external manifestations be forbidden; and in this way you will complete the revolution initiated by the study of philosophy, in this way you will be able—and without inflicting too violent a shock—to direct in the paths of reason the men whom you have been called upon to govern."[39] In conformity with the desires expressed by the recorder, the law forbade all external manifestations of the Faith, all public gatherings to which the ordinary citizen could be invited, all perpetual or life endowments destined for the Church's support.

Still more oppressive was the Law promulgated in 1871 by the Paris Commune. To get an idea of the spirit in which it was framed it is enough to glance at the preamble: "The Paris Commune . . . considering that the clergy have acted as accomplices in the crimes of the monarchy against liberty, decrees: Article I: The Church is separated from the State; Article II: The budget for public worship is suppressed." With a view to putting this measure into effect, the churches were closed, their sanctuaries profaned by shameless masquerades, whilst the priests were arrested and thrown into prison.

As regards the Law of 1905, this was passed in such an atmosphere of hatred and political passion that it can make no claim to be regarded as a liberal solution. As M. Ribot observed at the time, it was the work of a sectarian majority, resolved, not to liberate the Church but to attack her, to disorganize her, if possible to destroy her. Article IV in particular threatened all constitutional Catholic order: the *associations cultuelles* to which the administration of Church property and the supervision of religious worship was to be transferred were to be set up without reference to the hierarchy, of which the Law made no mention. These facts are sufficient to explain the energetic manner in which these laws were condemned by Pius X in the Encyclicals *Vehementer* of the 11th February, 1906, and *Gravissimo* of the 10th August, 1906.

France is not, however, the only country in which a policy of separatism, directed against the Church, has been put into effect. Since 1874, the Mexican Church has been separated from the State and has since then, on various occasions, been made the object of the most unfair discrimination at law. In Ecuador the Law of 1904 on religious worship limited in an objectionable manner the rights of religious orders to recruit new members. In Portugal, the Law of the 20th April, 1911, combined the principles of separatism with the most unreasonable features of the regalist ideology: tacitly a dead letter since 1926, this Law was legally abrogated by the Concordat of 1940. In Soviet Russia, to take a last instance, the Law of the 23rd January, 1918, which separated the Churches from the State, served merely to give a cloak of legality to a policy of violent and continuous persecution.[40]

Faced by these harsh realities, we must be careful not to draw too close a parallel between the liberal and separatist schools of thought. Separatism is a legal system which the State is free to apply in widely different manners. Since, under a separatist régime, the Church is no more than a society with private rights, an indifferentist or liberal government will subject her to the common law; a hostile or anti-clerical government will oppress her by means of vexatious police measures; a government favourable to religion will bestow upon her all manner of favours and privileges. Anything may happen, and all these experiments—as history bears witness—have in fact been tried out.

*      *      *

It is true, none the less, that in its historical origins separatism has been closely associated with the liberal ideal and has kept step with it in its various stages of development. In the eyes of liberalism, religion is a private, an individual affair, the Church being regarded not as a public institution but as a simple society of believers. A Church of that kind can clearly not be regarded as the perfect society, the competitor and rival of the temporal power, but neither can she be considered to be a mere chattel or tool of the State. Seen as a simple group of religious-minded persons, a Church of this sort is in no way dependent on the civil power and only asks of the latter to permit her to live on whatever conditions the maintenance of public order may require.

These new ideas were popularized in the sixteenth century by the *enfants terribles* of the Reformation, Anabaptists and dissidents of all types, even by those who—in opposition to the State Churches—upheld the rights of religious individualism. As early as Luther's day, the Anabaptists had begun to form communities of the elect, of "unspotted souls", living in isolation, aloof from the sinful world: baptism, administered only to adults, was the sign of interior conversion and of entry into this new life. The first sects of this kind, it is true, lapsed speedily into a sort of anarchic illuminism; but other communities of "Brethren", such as the Mennonites, were less formidable and underwent persecution at the hands of the official Churches.[41]

The same separatist tendencies sprang, in England, from opposition to the Established Church. Many complained indeed that they had only cast off the yoke of Rome to find themselves the victims of a severer despotism, that of a State-supported prelacy. On the left wing of the Puritan opposition the Congregationalist sect came into being in about 1560. The movement owed its vigour to Robert Browne who looked upon the Churches as independent societies, exempt from all control by the political authority. His ecclesiastical ideas could not indeed have been more individualistic. "A Church," he wrote, "is an association of Christians or of believers who, having freely entered upon an alliance with God, have placed themselves under the government of God and of Christ and keep

His laws in a holy bond of unity." The Church is thus regarded as a purely private society; it is not the State's business either to create or to maintain this society, which demands from it only liberty, or, at least, toleration.[42] Both in the case of Browne and, still more, in that of his disciples, numerous inconsistencies have been noted in the application of this separatist doctrine. Indeed at the time of the foundation of the first colonies in America, the Congregationalists who had settled in New England surpassed themselves in intolerance and, far from distinguishing between spiritual and temporal affairs, laid the foundations of a theocracy even more tyrannical than that of Calvin. The principles of Browne were not however forgotten and in Cromwell's days and in those of the Revolution, the Independents invoked them effectively in their fight against Puritan intolerance. In his numerous political writings, the famous author of *Paradise Lost* carried on a fierce campaign for the disestablishment of the Anglican Church. In 1654 Milton demanded that Cromwell should "leave the Church to the Church" and should "refuse to allow the two civil and secular powers, profoundly disparate as they were, to continue to pay court to each other and in reality to destroy one another, under the appearance of giving mutual aid".[43] Another controversialist of the period, John Goodwin, imbued as he was with religious individualism, impresses one as still more radical. According to him, the State must confine itself to the exercise of secular functions; it is in no way qualified to govern the Church any more than it is to define the foundations of orthodox belief. The idea of a national Church is a contradiction in terms. There are only Christian communities, little groups of regenerated souls in the midst of a sinful world. Goodwin proposed accordingly to extend a very wide degree of toleration to the sects, he was even prepared, in opposition to the general consensus of Anglican opinion, to apply it to the "Papists". "According to his theory," Herr Jordan has written, "the separation of Church and State is now complete and radical."[44]

Another English sect which resolutely defended the same principles was that of the Baptists. It owed its origin to the Anabaptists who emigrated to England from Holland in the

6*

period subsequent to 1559. After being persecuted for a long time, the sect came into prominence at the time of the Civil War. Amongst its theorists the best known is Roger Williams, who became famous as the founder of the colony of Rhode Island in America (1636). He returned on several occasions to England, where he published two books against the persecution of dissenters: *The Bloudy Tenent of Persecution* (1644) and *The Bloudy Tenent yet more Bloudy* (1652). No other contemporary work advocated more forcibly than these the complete separation of Church and State. Williams was an individualist who tried to be true to his principles. Salvation, he said, was a matter for individuals, not for Churches; the latter were merely voluntary associations of Christians intended to help on the work of personal salvation. There could be no national Church, this was a conception inherited from the Old Law but now obsolete. There was no State Church and it was dangerous to imagine that the security of the State could be dependent upon its religious unity. The State would be unable to fulfil its own purpose satisfactorily unless it devoted itself entirely to its secular activities, without troubling about the Churches and their divisions. Unlike the State, the Church resembled in all respects a professional association or guild:

> The Church or society of God's worshippers, be it true or false, is like a guild or college of physicians in a city, or a society of merchants doing commerce with the East Indies or Turkey. These societies can hold meetings, possess registers, organize debates; in those affairs which concern them, they can become disunited, divided, broken up into schisms and factions; they can summon each other before the courts, etc. . . . ; and yet the peace of the civil community and, in consequence, the conditions of its prosperity are essentially distinct from those of these individual guilds. The civil community is anterior to them, it remains intact and perfect, even if one guild or the other breaks up or is dissolved.[45]

Elsewhere Williams compared the Church and the State to two ships steering independent courses. In the first of these it is the Church that commands; the Prince is only a passenger and must submit himself to the discipline on board. In the

second the Prince gives the orders and the ministers of the
Church are strictly bound to obey him.[46] The traditional
liberal doctrine of the separation of Church and State could
scarcely be expressed more vividly than by these two similes—
that of the guild and that of the two ships.

The religious principles of the Baptists and of the Independents were restated at the end of the seventeenth century, in
the works of Locke: the Letter on Toleration (1689) and the
Treatise concerning Civil Government (1690). They are there
combined with that radical individualism which lay at the root
of Locke's philosophy. Civil society was, in his eyes, the outcome
of a contract prior to the conclusion of which men, living in
a state of nature, had enjoyed freedom and equality. This form
of existence, whilst imposing certain moral obligations upon
the individual had, in compensation, given him certain rights,
such as liberty of conscience, liberty to own property, the right
to take the law into one's own hands, etc. It was precisely the
difficulty met with in practice in exerting the last-named right
that impelled man to unite in a political society. The latter
was established not in order to absorb individual rights but in
order the better to defend them: all that individuals had to
do to attain to this end was to transfer to the hands of society
and of its government the right to judge and to punish; they
did not in this way make over their other natural rights, they
were on the contrary bound to see that they were safeguarded.
It will be observed that we are not far from the doctrine of
the Rights of Man as afterwards put forward by the Constituent
Assembly. It was thus, in any case, that Locke worked out the
theory of the liberal State, a State of which the functions were
reduced to the preservation of law and order, whilst its power
was limited on every side by the rights of the citizen.

Amongst these rights, freedom of conscience must be given
a high place. This cannot be lost through the contract, as the
citizen in fact makes over to the State only the right to punish injustice. Men therefore retain full liberty of conscience to associate
amongst themselves with a view to their salvation. So it is that
Churches are formed just as trade guilds or learned societies
are formed. They are totally independent of the State in regard
to their beliefs and internal discipline: an "established"

Church could not be set up except in violation of the contract. The State has no concern with sects even if they be given to idolatry, all it has to do is to make sure that they in no way threaten the political order. This last provision was used by Locke to justify the English laws against "Popery". Catholics were a danger to the security of the kingdom, he declared, because they obeyed, in the person of the Pope, a foreign sovereign. In this curious fashion he hoped to reconcile iniquitous laws with a most liberal theory of the relationship between Church and State.

*    *    *

In our account of separatist ideas, we have so far given pride of place to the rôle of the English theorists. The importance of the part played by these is easily explained by the religious state of Great Britain since the Reformation. In no other country have the sects increased and multiplied so steadily. In no other country has the strife between the nonconformists and the established Church been so bitter. This we can well understand in view of the rapid spread, in that insular country, of the main tenets of the liberal doctrine.

It was quite otherwise in the France of the *ancien régime*. As M. Mathiez has already pointed out, the idea of separating Church and State was almost a novelty in the milieux of the *philosophes*.[47] It is true that a certain infatuation for England and for liberal ideas prevailed in the France of the eighteenth century, but these ideas were usually applied only to matters concerning the art of government and it would not have occurred to the freethinkers of the period to put them into effect where matters of religion were concerned. Gallican regalism satisfied their lay conception of what authority should be, all the more because it assured to the State a profitable hold over spiritual things. "No empire can be wisely governed by two independent powers," said Helvetius. "There must not be two powers in a State," wrote Voltaire, "a wrong distinction is drawn between the temporal power and the spiritual power." So it was that the *philosophes* came to accept the universal competence of the civil authority in accordance with the formula of the Abbé Raynal: "The State is not made for religion, but religion for the State . . . When the State has spoken, the Church has nothing more to say."

Condorcet alone was gradually brought to accept the principles of separatism. The idea of complete religious toleration which he at first rejected eventually won his acceptance and, on the eve of the Revolution, he went so far as to prescribe for the State a policy of neutrality and religious indifference:[48]

> It has been to the advantage of princes [he wrote] not to endeavour to control religion but to separate religion from the State, allowing the priests to make free use of the sacraments, of censures and of ecclesiastical functions, without however giving any civil effect to their decisions. In all the countries in which the prince has interfered with religion, the State has been disturbed and the prince exposed to the attacks of fanatics, indeed only indifference about religion has succeeded in bringing about a lasting peace.

How is it that Condorcet, after having set out so clearly the principles of separatism, failed to show the uncompromising hostility to the Civil Constitution of the Clergy which might have been expected of him? The fact seems to be that, although in the course of his intrepid flights of intellect, he liked to beguile himself with pretty formulae regarding the progress of enlightenment and of the lay State, in practice he was a man of his age, both timorous and a time-server. At heart he remained true to the ideal which he had outlined in his books before the Revolution, for he expressed himself as follows in his personal notes on the 23rd March, 1792: "Let religion be separated once and for all from the civil order, let us be content to leave religion to the conscience only since it only concerns the conscience!" In his everyday political life as a journalist, he resigned himself to the Civil Constitution and salved his conscience by protesting against the exaggerated zeal of the *assermentés* when they attempted to identify their cause with that of the Revolution.

This attitude too should not surprise us. As M. Aulard has made clear, the idea of complete freedom of religious worship would at that period have found but little sympathy in France. It was only to a few minds that the schism resulting from the

Civil Constitution suggested the idea of disestablishing the Constitutional Church and neutralizing the State. The decree of the 7th May, 1791, which timidly authorized freedom of worship, was very badly received by the *sans-culottes*, and was soon as good as abrogated by the persecuting laws against refractory priests. Under the Legislative Assembly, only a few deputies and some authors spoke in favour of a separation on liberal lines. André Chénier was at first in favour of such a solution, but came to the conclusion that public opinion was not yet ripe for it. The Girondin Duclos advocated the idea with enthusiasm but the half-measure which was all that he actually proposed would have been difficult to apply and nothing came of it. The Abbé de Moy was the only one to table, on the 16th May, 1792, a really radical bill on the subject but this also was dropped. These facts make it easier to understand the hesitations of Condorcet in regard to a law of which he disapproved in principle but which was none the less definitely based upon a solid Gallican tradition.

The France of the eighteenth century never witnessed the spectacle familiar in Anglo-Saxon countries, of teeming rival sects. In spite of the presence of a Protestant minority, the French nation retained its Catholic unity, which even the freethinkers did not at first have any serious idea of breaking. Not only did they see in the Church a social safeguard—the people must have a religion!—but the domination of the Church by the State still seemed to them so desirable that, far from wishing to loosen this link, they thought that it needed tightening. Given this attitude towards politico-religious problems separatist doctrines could not expect, even in the France of the revolutionary period, to be given anything but a cold reception.

It was only in the United States of America, towards the end of the eighteenth century, that the separatist formula definitely won the day. Up to the time of the War of Independence (1776) the greatest diversity in religious government reigned in the British colonies. The severest of theocracies had held sway from the beginning in the New England States. Established Churches controlled religious life in Virginia and Carolina. The State of Maryland, founded in 1634 by George Calvert, afterwards Lord Baltimore, was at first a place of

refuge for a Catholic majority and for some years enjoyed
complete religious toleration. Puritan and Anglican immigra-
tion led, however, to the overthrow of the majority, and this
meant a renewal of intolerance; indeed, from the end of the
seventeenth century, an Anglican State Church repaid the
Catholic dissidents for their previous kindness by persecuting
them for their faith. Two States alone remained more or less
faithful to the principle of freedom of worship, the colony of
Rhode Island founded in 1634 by Roger Williams and that of
Pennsylvania, founded in 1681 by the Quaker William Penn—
neither of these States possessing established Churches. This
is by no means a brilliant record of tolerance, however, especially when one considers the scale and number of the
protestations raised against the Church of England by the
dissenting sects of the mother-country.

It was the War of Independence which served to put an
end to this diversity. The dearly-won union of the American
States availed more than any number of theories to secure
the extension to the whole nation of the separatist system.
Article VI of the Federal Constitution laid down, in sharp
contrast to the provisions of British Law, that "no religious
oath would ever be required as a condition of filling an office
or public function in the name of the United States." Amend-
ment I added that "Congress could pass no law relative to the
establishment of a religion or prohibiting the free exercise of
any one of them". One after another, the various States proceeded to disestablish the dominant Churches. There were no
grave difficulties, only certain delays. Massachusetts, where
Puritan intolerance had so long held sway, only consummated
the work of separation in 1833. Since then, the various Churches
of America, amongst them the Catholic Church, have been
organized on the principle of liberty of association which,
interpreted in a wide sense, is loyally respected by the public
authorities.

*          *          *

During the nineteenth century, the progress of the doctrine
of separation went hand in hand with the development of
liberalism in all domains, religious, political and economic;

and we find the separation of Church and State demanded simultaneously—though for very different reasons—by religious individualists, by liberal politicians, and by some liberal Catholics.

As we have already remarked, religious individualism, an inevitable result of the Reformation, made itself felt at an early stage in the dissenting sects, Congregationalist or Baptist. It gained a much wider foothold in the course of the nineteenth century under the name of "liberal Protestantism". The latter, regarding religion as a purely subjective matter, reduced the rôle of the Churches to that of simple associations of believers and demanded no legal privileges for them. Even in Germany, where the hold of the State over religion was so strong, some theologians persistently advocated a separatist policy; one of the most illustrious amongst them, Friedrich Schleiermacher, was a pioneer in the cause of liberal Protestantism. It was, however, in French-speaking countries that the principles of separatism found their most enthusiastic champions. They were literally converted into dogma by the Swiss author Alexandre Vinet in his *Essai sur la manifestation des convictions religieuses* (1839). Vinet's whole purpose was to demonstrate that civil society, as such, cannot have any religion and that it has no authority to concern itself with ecclesiastical denominations, even with a view to their defence. In fact, he says, one must choose between two things: either society has a religion and the individual has not; or else it is the individual who has a religion, in which case society cannot have one.

If society has a religion this means that society has a conscience; and if society has a conscience, how could the individual conscience prevail against that of society? Conscience is supreme in man, how should it not be supreme in society? Strong in his individual conscience, a man is capable of opposing society; what sort of figure would a man cut in opposition to a society which, *qua* society, had a conscience of its own? It is impossible to oppose supremacy to supremacy, omnipotence to omnipotence, it is impossible to suppose that, from all the individual consciences of men, with all their diversity, a social conscience can result. What mystery, or rather what absurdity, is here being suggested to us? No, if society has a conscience, this can only be on the condition that an individual has none, and since conscience is the seat of religion, it follows that, if society is religious, the individual is not.[49]

Now everything, Vinet continues, combines to prove to us the purely individual character of religion. Religion is a conviction, a sentiment; it is necessary then that it should remain individual, "for it can only be experienced as religion by the individual". No doubt it has its social aspect, it tends to become a Church: "but in this entirely spiritual society, the individual never abdicates his throne; for such is a necessary condition of existence for this society which is only a religious society or church in so far as adhesion to it is spontaneous, separation being always possible and constraint impossible."[50] Vinet resolves the dilemma thus: "Religion is an individual matter, it is apart from civil society; the State has no cognizance of Churches except as private societies to be treated, like other such societies, in accordance with the rules of common law." No one had ever before linked so closely the idea of separatism with the postulates of individualism in the religious field.

Vinet has found many followers amongst Swiss and French Protestants, especially in the days since the Second Empire. Edmond de Pressensé and the philosopher Charles Secretan must be counted amongst his most enthusiastic disciples. Even whole communities have been won over. The *Conférences nationales évangeliques* (southern section) passed, in their Assembly of 1871, a resolution favourable to the principle of separation and although one cannot conclude from this that the Law of 1905 met with the general approval of French Protestants it does at least show that it was in accordance with the essential tendencies of its liberal left wing.

\* \* \*

In the nineteenth century the separation of Church and State became one of the favourite slogans of political liberalism. We must of course distinguish between the two separate schools which, since the Restoration, had borne the label "Liberal". One of these, originally represented by the *Constitutionel*,

6\*\*

remained faithful to revolutionary principles and Gallican maxims; it was liberal only in name and, under colour of observing the Concordat, continued to heap difficulties upon the Church. The other school of theorists, who had the *Globe* as their organ and admired greatly the British and American constitutions, was forever bringing pressure to bear on the State to grant all the individual liberties: liberty of opinion, of the press and of public worship. Themselves unbelievers or indifferentists, men of this school hoped none the less that a loyal and complete separation would bring with it a solution of the difficulties pending between Church and State. Jouffroy made fun of those pretended Liberals who badgered Jesuits or missionaries and boasted of having forced the Church to agree to a religious funeral for an atheist: "It is said [he wrote] that the *dévots* try to fit the State into the Church; unbelievers desire the Church to be in the State. It does not seem to occur to anyone that the Church, which is a *belief*, has nothing to do with the State which is a material force."[51] And Dubois, another writer in the *Globe*, was all in favour of concrete solutions, suppressing the budget for religious affairs, and neutralizing the State. "Need it be so long," he wrote, "until the maintenance of each Church can be left to its own adherents and until the administration of its funds, like the truth of its doctrines, can be left in the hands of its own functionaries? Need we regard as rash the peaceful idea of separating the State for ever from religion and of maintaining it unchanging and unmoved amidst the reforms and passions of theology?"[52]

After 1830 and throughout the nineteenth century we continue to be aware of these two political tendencies, but it is the first of the two, the less favourable to liberty, which undoubtedly has the upper hand. In the time of Jules Ferry we find a true Liberal, in the person of Jules Simon, noting the fact with sorrow.

There is no need for the moment [he wrote in 1883[53]] to worry about the separatists, they are on the down-grade. The dominant Church (I refer to the Church of the unbelievers) is, on the other hand, full of enthusiasm about the Concordat; all they regret is that it is not carried out in every detail. Far from loosing the links of Church and State, these men want to draw them tighter. The Church, they say, would not be able to complain, and the Republican State could not wish for a better school than that of Bonaparte in which to consolidate its authority.

Notorious anti-clericals like Renouvier, Gambetta, Paul Bert or Charles Ferry were too conscious of the advantages of regalism to be ready to accept with open arms a liberal policy. Even the Radicals were only willing to rally to separatism on condition that it should be interpreted in their own sense as a policy which would discriminate against the Church in favour of the State.

None the less, genuine liberalism could always be sure of finding determined adherents in the world of politics. Whether or not they favoured Catholicism, these men believed that the best way of obtaining a peaceful settlement of religious disputes lay in the complete neutralization of the State. Certain of the early Liberals, it is true, retracted their opinions after 1830, amongst these being Dubois who was disquieted by the press campaign of the *Avenir* or by the religious revival in Belgium. But, once it had made itself felt, the tendency towards separatism persisted and, in the early days of the July monarchy, Lamartine and the lawyer Nachet continued, together with the Catholics of the *Avenir*, to advocate this solution. Some years later, Tocqueville commended the idea in his work on democracy in America.[54] In the time of the Second Republic, in addition to Quinet, whose hatred of the Church led him to advocate separation, we find the political economist Bastiat giving it his approval both on economic and on religious grounds.[55] Under the Empire, politicians and philosophers such as Nefftzer (founder of *Le Temps*), Edouard Laboulaye, Jules Vacherot, Prévost-Paradol and Jules Simon likewise became the apostles and apologists of the separatist idea. Finally, in the Combes period, we find such men as Henry Maret, René Goblet, Raymond Poincaré, Emile Flourens, and there were others, advocating a separation on friendly terms and of a kind which could not be used by those in power as a weapon with which to attack religion.

Outside France, Liberal politicians did not usually view the separatist idea with any enthusiasm. In England, in the time of Gladstone, after the disestablishment of the Protestant Church of Ireland (1869) some voices were raised in favour of more radical measures, but they met with but little support. German Liberalism was almost equally unfavourable to the disestablishment idea. In Italy, on the other hand, the founder of the national unity, made brilliant use of the celebrated formula: "A free Church in a free State", and indeed, as M. Giacometti [56] has proved, Cavour had fallen when young under the influence of Vinet's theories. As far back as 1840, he had entered into relations with the French Liberals, notably Tocqueville, whose work on America he had greatly admired. We can thus see that he was won over in good time to the idea of separation, and events in Italy, in which he subsequently played so prominent a part, enabled him to further his political plans by popularizing these views. What was in fact his object? It was nothing less than to induce the Pope to relinquish his temporal power. From about 1860 onwards, Cavour tried to persuade Pius IX of the advantages of this solution, and he assured the Pope that, at the cost of this radical self-spoliation, he would be able to enjoy in peace full spiritual independence. If he gave up all claim to earthly dominion, the Italian State, for its part, would henceforth refrain from any interference in the affairs of the Church. It will be enough to recall the following typical passage, in a speech made by Cavour to the Chamber on the 27th March, 1861: [57]

Holy Father, the temporal power is no longer a guarantee of independence for you: if you will renounce it we will give you that liberty which for three centuries you have demanded in vain from the great Catholic Powers; that liberty of which you have tried to obtain some shreds for yourself by means of concordats which forced you in exchange to grant certain privileges and, even worse than these privileges, the use of spiritual arms to those temporal powers which allowed you a little liberty. Well, what you have never been able to obtain of powers who boast themselves to be your allies and devoted sons, we now offer you in all its plenitude, we are ready to proclaim in Italy the great principle: A free Church in a free State.

Montalembert has taken a severe view of these audacious proposals. On Cavour's lips the famous formula which he had been the first to employ and which summed up his own political ideas seemed to Montalembert to have acquired a new and distorted significance. "It is not a free Church in a free State that they are offering us," he cried, "it is a despoiled Church in a State of despoilers!"[58] Modern historians, M. Charles Benoist, for example, have however taken a more indulgent view, and there seems no doubt that they are right. Cavour had but little use for concordats; he saw in them a system of reciprocal encroachments by Church and State. For these outworn formulae he desired, in his liberal optimism, to substitute another which he thought would serve true spiritual interests better. He was truly convinced of its value and, shortly before he died, it recurred to his mind. "*Frate*," he said to the good friar who stood by his deathbed, "*libera Chiesa in libero Stato* "[59]

One of Cavour's collaborators, Signor Minghetti, went further than he did in his projects for a separation of Church and State. His book *Stato e Chiesa* (1878) seems to have been inspired by excellent intentions. "We hear tell of a juridical separation," he wrote, "which by no means excludes moral union." He began by assimilating the Church to a society governed by common law. Then, led astray by his democratic prejudices, he called for the election by the people of their spiritual heads and for the participation of the faithful in the government of Christian communities: that is to say—as Mgr. d'Hulst has pointed out—whilst professing to wash his hands of the religious society, he took upon himself to modify its constitution.[60]

*      *      *

It remains for us to define the attitude of Liberal Catholics in regard to the problem of separation. None of them of course ever accepted as valid the assumptions on which religious individualism and belief in the lay State are based. Lamennais himself, in the year 1830, laid down as a fundamental principle the Catholic thesis: "The religious and civil societies, Church and State, are by nature inseparable; they should be united like body and soul, and in that order."[61] Such is the traditional

doctrine and one that has never been called in question by
Liberal Catholics. We may even add that, after the condemnation of the *Avenir*, the latter for some time adopted a cautious
attitude in regard to the separation question. They may sometimes, without taking sufficient thought, have advocated an
accommodation between the Church and the modern freedoms:
freedom of conscience, freedom of the press and freedom of
worship. Only a few have been in favour of the rupture of the
Concordat and of the relegation of the Church to the position
of a private society. Such was the attitude taken up by Lamennais
in 1830 when, indignant at the enslavement of the Church to
secular domination, he was unable to see any salvation for her
except through a total and immediate separation. 62

> We Catholics demand the total separation of Church and
> State . . . This necessary separation, failing which no
> religious liberty would exist for Catholics, involves on the
> one hand, as we have fully recognized, the suppression of the
> ecclesiastical budget; on the other hand, the absolute
> independence of the clergy in the spiritual order, though of
> course the priest will remain subject to the laws of the
> country, to the same extent and in the same degree as other
> citizens. In consequence, the Charter being the first law,
> and liberty of conscience the first right of Frenchmen, we
> regard as definitely null and void any given law which is
> opposed to the Charter and incompatible with the rights
> and liberties which it proclaims; and hence we hold that it
> is the Government's duty to come to an agreement with
> the Pope, and that without any delay, with a view to the
> abrogation by mutual consent of a Concordat which has
> become impossible of execution ever since, thanks be to
> God, the Catholic religion has ceased to be the State
> religion. Just as there can to-day be nothing of religion in
> politics, so there must be nothing of politics in religion.

Montalembert and Lacordaire may have found themselves
for a time in sympathy with this radical point of view, but after
the revolt of Lamennais against the Holy See they came to
realize its regrettable laicist implications. In his celebrated
speeches at Malines, on the 20th and 21st August, 1863,
Montalembert showed greater reserve. These speeches, as is

well known, were not beyond criticism. The second particularly—on liberty of worship—contained certain declarations
which even the orator's best friends judged imprudent. He
was however careful not to reproduce in undiluted form the
demands formerly put forward in the *Avenir*.[63]

The reciprocal independence of Church and State, which
is the guiding principle of modern societies, does not by any
means involve their complete separation from one another,
still less their mutual hostility. Such complete separation is
by no means an essential condition of religious or public
liberty. On the contrary, it can very well bring with it, as
we see from the French Revolution, a savage oppression of
both. A free Church in a free State does not at all imply a
Church at war with the State, or a Church hostile or foreign
to the State. Church and State are able, nay, bound to come
to an agreement in order to reconcile mutual interests and
to afford, alike to society and to the individual, the advantages which only such an agreement can obtain for them.
There should be between the two a possible, legitimate and
often necessary alliance, which can and must be serious and
durable, but of which their independence in regard to one
another and the autonomy of each is an indispensable
condition.

In fact, after the crisis of 1830, the Liberal Catholics did not
again for a long time demand the abrogation of the Concordat.
Their organ, *Le Correspondant*, offers us a proof of this. Thus,
on the 10th December, 1849, the editors permitted the inclusion
in the review of an article favouring separation, but a pre-
liminary note warned readers that the article was not in
conformity with accepted doctrine and that its author,
M. Metz-Noblat, was not a member of the editorial staff.
Later on, towards the end of the Second Empire, when Jules
Simon, in his address to the Legislative body on the 3rd
December, 1867, urged Catholics to break the bonds of the
Concordat, this proposal was left unheeded. Under the Third
Republic, Anatole Leroy-Beaulieu, in his book on Liberal
Catholics (1885), described the campaign of the *Avenir* in favour
of separation[64] as showing extreme temerity. The same author
criticized the proposed solution severely in an article in the

*Revue des Deux Mondes* of the 15th April, 1886. "The separation of Church and State," he concluded, "would be for the Republic its revocation of the Edict of Nantes."

It was only towards the end of the century that a certain number of Catholics of all shades of opinion, liberal and conservative, began to envisage a radical solution. They were revolted by the spectacle of the exploitation of the Concordat by an irreligious and anti-clerical government and in consequence some came to think of a breach between the Church of France and the State as the lesser of two evils. These new ideas could not have been better expressed than in the words of Mgr. d'Hulst who wrote on the 15th December, 1895:[65]

> I have the impression that we are entering upon a difficult period for the French Church. We are going in the direction of separation, of a rupture of the Concordat, and I cannot bring myself to regret the fact, for I am convinced that it has rendered all the services that it was capable of rendering and that it no longer does us anything but harm. But, as this rupture is sure to be preceded by legislative measures intended to deprive us of our liberty in advance, what we have to expect is suffering, and that for a long while. So be it! the rotten fruit will fall away beneath the tempest's onslaught and the spirit of clergy and people alike will be dipped again into the bitter waters of healing. I hope to see this happen before I die.

Liberal Catholics, then, have played but a limited part in the modern separatist movement. They were tending no doubt —more or less consciously—in that direction when they welcomed too indulgently the individualist doctrines of the Revolution. But except for the small *Avenir* group they regarded with mistrust the proposed religious policy of the Liberal school. Not only did they reject its principles, they were even unwilling to give it any support in practice. It was indeed only in a mood of war-weariness and prescinding from all matters of doctrinal controversy that some Catholics felt able to accept the separatist solution as the lesser of two evils.

It is true then to say that such satisfactory results as have been achieved on separatist lines have been dictated less by principles than by practical considerations. In the United States, as we

have seen, it was the need for a truly united nation—both
during and after the American Revolution—which forced the
separatist solution upon Churches and sects. At Geneva (1907)
and at Basle (1910) separation between Church and State was
rendered necessary by the great access of Catholic immigrants
into these Protestant Cantons. That the principles of Vinet
had but little to do with this was unwillingly admitted by
Pastor Picot. "This law," he wrote, "is to be regarded more
as a victory for the ultramontanes and the enemies of all
religion than as a triumph for the principles of religious liberty.
It is not so much Vinet as Voltaire and Mermillod who have
won the day."[66] In Brazil the separation between Church and
State was brought about by the Republic in 1891 and cannot
be regarded as signifying the triumph of a dominant ideology,
being rather in the nature of a compromise between the
Liberals, as believers in State "regalism", and the Catholics
and Positivists combined. In Chile the Law of Separation,
passed in 1925, was certainly not solely due to liberal ideas
for, in that country, the Church, far from being made completely subject to the common law, enjoys various privileges
with which the Holy See has declared itself satisfied.[67]

Since the days of Gregory XVI,[68] separatist principles have
been condemned on many occasions by the Roman Pontiffs.
There is no reason to be surprised at this, for not only do they
contradict the traditional teaching of the Church, they also
involve grave errors as to the mission of civil society and the
nature of religion. As we have seen, it was from the religious
individualists that the separatist idea first sprang. The Baptist
and Congregationalist sects and the Liberal Protestants
championed it logically enough, as the direct consequence of
their basic teachings. If, indeed, all religion is an individual
affair and the Churches are no more than free associations of
believers, there cannot, of course, be any spiritual sovereignty
opposed to that of the State. In that case, the Church must no
longer be regarded as a visible and independent institution
who owes both her foundation and her continued existence to
the Will of Christ; she becomes merely a "friendly society",
subject like the rest to the provisions of the Common Law.
On liberal premisses, this is quite logical but it is a complete

reversal of the Catholic position, for it means that instead of a sovereign Church which draws men to her allegiance, we have nothing but individuals who group themselves into Churches under the aegis of an indifferent or favourable temporal power.

The separatist doctrines are also based on another error, that which pushes the secularization of the State to the point at which it becomes entirely indifferent to all religion. Such an attitude as this is contrary to the Church's teaching on the mission of the State for, although confined to the temporal order, the State is none the less concerned with the spiritual ends of the human community: these it is bound to presuppose and to these its other aims must be subordinated. Indeed, if the political power tries to ignore on principle the existence of these higher ends, it risks placing serious obstacles in their way.

> This thesis [Pius X declared] is an evident negation of the supernatural order. It in fact confines the action of the State solely to the pursuit of the prosperity of the community in this present life . . . and, as though the matter in no way concerned it, it pays no attention whatsoever to the final end of man, namely the eternal happiness to which he can attain after his brief life on earth is concluded. And yet, since the present order of things is limited to time and is thus subordinate to the conquest of that superior and absolute good, the civil power is bound not only to refrain from placing obstacles in the way of our attaining that good but also to help us to attain it. [69]

If the legislator, even without hostile intent, thinks fit to ignore the life of the spirit, he will easily embark upon a course liable to threaten both the independence of the Church and that of the faithful. Recognizing no authority but his own, he will, in practice, behave like a man who is blind or unaware of the true significance of his own acts; he will trample, without even being aware of the fact, on the most elementary rights of the Christian conscience.

Separatist principles can in short lead only to misconceptions. Relegating the Church to the precarious position of a private society, they make the liberty of the spiritual power dependent on the goodwill of the temporal authorities. From this point they proceed, in practice, to disparate and contradictory solutions: subjection to the common law, or privileged treatment, or persecution. How could the Church express approval of so glaringly ambiguous a solution? It is not upon a foundation of this sort that a coherent doctrine of the relations between Church and State can be erected.

So far as principles are concerned, we must then admit the incompatibility of separatism and the Catholic doctrine. In the mind of the Holy See the distinction drawn between the two powers is of a nature which necessarily implies their mutual co-operation. But the Holy See—realistic as always—is here thinking less of formal agreements than of reciprocal sympathy and solid mutual goodwill. As M. Le Bras neatly put it, "Concord, rather than concordats, is what the Church preaches". The same eminent canonist has also pointed out that there are such things as "stormy concordats and cordial separations".[70] In the hands of a hostile and tyrannical power, a concordat can be a dangerous weapon. On the other hand, whilst separation can be an excuse for persecution, some separations have begun by being friendly and others have become so. The situation in law does not always reflect the true nature of relations between two powers: sometimes it is in contradiction to them. Pius XI, as we have seen, pointed this out in a happy phrase when he described the separation in Chile as a "friendly union". Thus, although hostile to separatism on grounds of principle, the Papacy is sometimes ready, for grave reasons, to approve it in practice. Pius XI, in spite of his fondness for concordats, expressed no disapproval of other existing solutions of the problem. This was because, in such countries as the United States, Brazil, Switzerland and Chile, separation was not brought about under pressure from the exponents of any particular theory or ideology but was imposed as an effective means of ensuring civic and religious peace. Applied in a sense favourable to the hierarchy, separation on this basis safeguards that moral union and that goodwill which, in the eyes of the Holy See, are the essential *desiderata*. Pius X himself made it sufficiently clear that he would have resigned himself to the Law of Separation if it had not placed

the Church of France in an intolerable position. "Since,"
he said, "the State chose by breaking the bonds of the Concordat, to separate itself from the Church, it ought, as a natural
consequence, to have left her with her independence and to have
permitted her to enjoy in the peace of the common law the
liberty which it professed to be giving her."[71] As a result of
conciliatory legislation and a modification of the bias against
the hierarchy from which it originally suffered, the religious
situation established in 1905 later on became more acceptable,
a fact recognized by Pius XI when, in 1924, he recommended
the French bishops to form diocesan associations. Eventually
the separation of Church and State was placed on a new footing
by a tacit understanding and by the exchange of diplomatic
representatives as a result of which the relations between
France and the Holy See have now become markedly cordial
in character. We accordingly see how true it is that—whatever
may be said about concordats and separatism—solid proofs
of loyal friendships are what the Church prizes above all.

### NOTES TO CHAPTER VIII

[1] *De potestate regia et papali*, C.1 and 4; edited J. Leclercq, *Jean de Paris et l'ecclésiologie du XIIIe siècle*, Paris, 1942, pp. 176–178, 182–183.

[2] *Ricordi politici e civili*, n.142 in *Opera medite*, Vol. I, Florence, 1867, p. 136.

[3] The text of these instructions has been included by M. de Boüard in his study, *La Légation du Cardinal Caetani en France* (1589–1590), Bordeaux, 1932, cf. p. 62.

[4] Text in Le Plat, *Monumenta ad historiam concilii tridentini spectantia*, Vol. I, Louvain, 1783, p. 185.

[5] B. Arroy, *Questions décidées sur la justice des armes du roi de France*, Paris, 1934, q. 4, p. 190.

[6] J. Gaufridy, *L'Impiété renversée*, Paris, 1636, p. 35.

[7] *Mercure français*, Vol. XI (1625), pp. 1089–1090.

[8] Davenport, *European treaties bearing on the History of the United States and its Dependencies*, Washington, 1917, p. 220, No. 9.

[9] Michel de l'Hospital, *Œuvres*, published by Dufey, Paris, 1824, I, p. 398.

10 *Des Etats Généraux*, Paris, 1789, XII, pp. 234–236.

11 *Œuvres*, I, p. 478.

12 Manifesto quoted by F. de Crue, *Le Parti des Politiques*, Paris, 1892, p. 294.

13 *Œuvres*, I, p. 396.

14 *Exhortation aux Princes*, in the *Mémoires de Condé*, Paris edition, 1743, II, pp. 614, 621, 635.

15 *Œuvres*, II, pp. 193, 196.

16 J. Bodin, *La République*, III, 7, Paris edition, 1577, p. 583.

17 *Bulletin historique du Protestantisme français*, Vol. II, 1853, pp. 132–133—Speech delivered by the King, 16 February, 1599.

18 *Lettres du Cardinal de Richelieu*, edition d'Avenel, I, p. 224.

19 In his book *Richelieu*.

20 L. Lallemant, *Doctrine spirituelle*, 4th section, Ch. 4, a. 2: published by Potier, Paris, 1936, p. 182.

21 P. Vermeersch, *La Tolérance*, Paris, 1922, pp. 214–216.

22 F. Meinecke, *Die Idee der Staatsräson in der Neueren Geschichte*, Berlin, 1929, pp. 58 *et seq.*

23 *Maximes d'Etat*, nos. 80 and 124; published by Hanotaux in the collection of *Documents inédits*, Mélanges historiques, III, pp. 770, 784.

24 *Le Catholique d'Etat*, in Hay du Chastelet, *Recueil de diverses pièces pour servir à l'histoire*, edition of 1640, pp. 95, 123, 820.

25 *Recueil des plus générales considérations servant au maniement des affaires publiques*, Bibl. nat. fonds fr., 19048, pp. 439–440.

26 *Aristippe*, 6th discourse, in *Œuvres* (Moreau), II, pp. 234–235.

27 *Apologie*, quoted by R. Celeste, *C. Machon, Nouvelles Recherches sur sa vie et ses œuvres*, Bordeaux, 1883, pp. 58–59.

28 *Considérations politiques sur les Coups d'Etat*, Rome, 1639, pp. 59, 65, 71, 110, 114.

29 *Les six livres de la République*, I, 9; 1577 edition, p. 188.

30 *Op. cit.*, II, 2, p. 351.

31 *Histoire générale du Droit français*, Paris, 1925, p. 444.

32 *Traité de la Souveraineté*, Ch.IX, in *Œuvres*, Paris edition, 1689, p. 18.

33 *Traité de l'Autorité Royale*, Paris, 1691, p. 518. Cf. J. Hitier, *La Doctrine de l'Absolutisme*, Paris, 1902, pp. 82–88.

34 *Op. cit.* Ch.XII, p. 25.

35 *Œuvres*, Paris, 1759, XIII, p. 330.

36 As regards these two theories—Episcopalism and Territorialism—cf. K. Rieker, *Die rechtliche Stellung der evangelischen Kirche Deutschlands*, Leipzig, 1893, pp. 208 *et seq.*

37 E. Ollivier, *L'Eglise et l'Etat au Concile du Vatican*, I, p. 95.

38 Lamennais, *Troisièmes Mélanges*, Paris, 1835, p. 114 (article which appeared in the *Avenir*, 18th October, 1830–   ).

[39] An analysis of this Report and extracts from it are to be found in M. Bérard, *Essai historique sur la Séparation de l'Eglise et l'Etat pendant la Révolution*, Paris, 1906, pp. 138–160.

[40] The texts of these different Separation Laws may be found in Giacometti, *Quellen zur Geschichte der Trennung von Staat und Kirche*, Tübingen, 1926, pp. 412, 424, 429, 436.

[41] K. Rothenbücher, *Die Trennung von Staat und Kirche*, Munich, 1908, pp. 23–28.

[42] On R. Browne and the Congregationalist movement, see K. Jordan, *The Development of Religious Toleration in England*, Vol. I, London, 1932, pp. 261–295.

[43] *Secunda Defensio pro Populo anglicano*, in *Historical and Political Works of J. Milton*, London, 1738, II, p. 347. As regards Milton's liberal ideas, cf. M. Freund, *Die Idee der Toleranz in England der grossen Revolution*, Halle, 1927, pp. 145–200.

[44] K. Jordan, *op. cit.*, III, p. 384; cf. Freund, *op. cit.*, pp. 202 *et seq.*

[45] *The Bloudy Tenent of Persecution* (Caldwell edition), p. 46.

[46] *Ibid.*, pp. 399–400. On Roger Williams, cf. the two works named by Jordan (III, pp. 472–506), and by Freund (pp. 241–267).

[47] *Revue historique*, 1910, Vol. CIII, pp. 63–79.

[48] *Œuvres*, published by O'Connor and Arago, IV, pp. 538–539.

[49] *Essai sur la manifestation des convictions religieuses*, New edition, Paris, 1928, pp. 211–212.

[50] *Op. cit.*, pp. 219–220.

[51] Quoted by P. Thureau-Dangin, *Le Parti libéral sous la Restauration*, Paris, 1888, p. 371.

[52] *Fragments littéraires*, Paris, 1879, II, p. 34.

[53] J. Simon, *La Liberté de Conscience*, 6th edition, Preface, p. xx.

[54] *La Démocratie en Amérique*, Paris, 1874, II, pp. 222 *et seq.*

[55] F. Bastiat, *Ebauches*, n.78, 80, in *Œuvres Complètes*, Paris, 1864, VII, pp. 351, 360.

[56] In his work *Die Genesis von Cavours Formel*, Libera Chiesa in libero Stato, Zurich, 1910.

[57] Cf. M. Charles Benoist (in the *Revue des Deux Mondes*, 15 July, 1905), *L'Eglise libre dans l'Etat libre*, pp. 344–345.

[58] Montalembert, *L'Eglise libre dans l'Etat libre*. Address delivered at the Congress of Malines, Paris, 1863, p. 180.

[59] *Art.cit.*, p. 372.

[60] *Carême*, 1895, p. 391.

[61] *Avenir*, 18 October, 1830. *Troisièmes Mélanges*, Paris, 1835, p. 110.

[62] *Avenir*, 7 December, 1830. *Troisièmes Mélanges*, pp. 159–161.

[63] *L'Eglise libre dans l'Etat libre*, pp. 142–143.

[64] A. Leroy-Beaulieu, *Les Catholiques Libéraux*, p. 96.

[65] Quoted by Cardinal Baudrillart, *Vie de Mgr. d'Hulst*, II, p. 436.

[66] A. Chavan, *La Séparation de l'Eglise et de l'Etat, d'après Alexandre Vinet* in the *Revue d'Histoire et de Littérature religieuses*, 1924, p. 550.

67 *Acta Apostolicae Sedis*, 1925, p. 642.
68 Encyclical *Mirari vos* (15 August, 1832).
69 Encyclical *Vehementer*.
70 *Trente Ans de Séparation* in the collection *Chiesa e Stato*, Studi storici e giuridici per il decennale della Conciliazione tra la Santa Sede e l'Italia, Milan, 1939, II, p. 462.
71 Encyclical *Vehementer*.

# CONCLUSION

Our Lord Jesus Christ came to reveal to mankind the mysteries of the Divine Life and the plans of God's Redeeming Love. This message, despite its purely spiritual character, none the less gave rise to a profound and lasting revolution in the government of human society. The foundation of the Church—the custodian of the Divine message —separated in the ancient State two elements which had hitherto been united, namely the civil authority and the religious authority. By creating a Church which was autonomous in its own sphere, Christ Our Lord established in the world a dual sovereignty. This dualism was to be but relative, because—according to Catholic doctrine—it did not involve the radical separation of the two authorities but rather their peaceful collaboration. None the less it was to be permanent, for the spiritual power, in spite of its primacy, had not the right to abolish dualism or turn it to its own advantage.

Experience has shown that dualism is not easy to maintain in practice. As we have pointed out in the second part of the present study, everything seems to combine in a sort of permanent conspiracy against it. The struggle began in the early days of the Church. The Roman Empire had recourse to a bloody persecution in order to defend its absolute sovereignty against the new religion. After the Peace of Milan, Caesaro-papism became, in Rome and still more at Byzantium, the permanent temptation of the Christian Emperors. In the Middle Ages it was the Church which allowed herself to be captured in her turn by the mirage of unity. Certain theologians were heard to declare that a Christendom with two heads would be a monster, and even a Pope echoed their opinions. It was no longer enough for these men to place at the head of the Christian order Christ Himself, sole Priest and King. They claimed that His universal primacy had been delegated in all its completeness to His representative on earth. Since the Renaissance period, the renewed preponderance of the State led to a swing-back of the passion for absolute sovereignty to the secular side. The outworn formulae of Caesaro-papism were replaced by the still more despotic claims of modern regalism, the completely secular and entirely unchecked domination of the doctrine of national expediency. The separatist error itself is really based essentially upon the assumption that sovereignty is indivisible and that the Church is only a private society in the sovereign State.

The study of the age-long struggle against dualism furnishes us with arguments in its defence. In so far as these efforts have succeeded, they carry with them their own condemnation. During the last thousand years in particular, the western world has tried, in politics, two major experiments. There has been the medieval experiment, that of a civilization built by the Church—under her direction and her supremacy. No one can deny the magnificence of this achievement or the splendour of its successes. But nor can one avoid noting its disappointing features: we see the Church embarrassed with temporal cares, the Papacy obsessed by financial questions and political difficulties, Christendom eventually lapsing into a deplorable state of torpor from which it was to be aroused by the thunderclap of the Reformation. Then, during the last four centuries, we have seen the modern experiment: the rise to power of the national States, the establishment in their respective territories of national and centralized governments, the prodigious development of science and mechanics. It is impossible to deny the brilliance of this achievement or its beneficent effect in many spheres of human activity. This temporal progress has had to be paid for, however, by the insatiable ambition of the secular sovereignty, by the fatal effect which laicism has had on the religious sense, by the claim of the State to control and to absorb everything, and finally by the most rigorous and the most unbridled absolutism. We have much to learn from this twofold experiment. It seems to show that a nation cannot be caught in the vice of a single authority without great risk both to the liberty of the human person and to the harmonious development of civilization.

To however great an extent it may be justified both by the lessons of history and by present circumstances, dualism is nevertheless not by itself sufficient, for it leaves our minds restless and unsatisfied. We are thus able to understand how all along the ages a contrary movement has made itself felt—an irresistible tendency towards unity. The very separation of things spiritual from things temporal seems to suggest a certain instability, a lack of final achievement! It calls for a *dénouement*, a final synthesis which will reconcile opposites. If we view things from a Christian point of view it would appear to be the destiny of the spiritual society to bring about some day the desired consummation. Even at the present day, it is the spiritual which has the pre-eminence and which claims the primacy. A day will come when all temporary distinctions affecting the Body of Christ will pass away and everything will be fulfilled in unity.

But when are we to expect this goal to be reached—here below or only in a better world? Are we to suppose, for instance, that the progress of Christianity will one day render it unnecessary for us men, even whilst yet on earth, to retain the duality of Church and State? Can it be that the Church will be called upon to build, even in this world, the complete City of God, freed from the passing limitations which still make manifest its imperfect condition? This may have been believed in the Middle Ages; indeed the efforts of medieval civilization were directed towards a unique and perfect Christendom in which the civil power would be no more than the instrument of the spiritual power. St. Augustine was less ambitious. The City of God about which he told us is not destined to reach its completion on this earth. It must travel until the end of time on its long and toilsome pilgrimage. Here below it must tend, although it may never attain to them, towards justice and towards peace. The reciprocal limitations from which the two powers suffer is one of the marks of our temporal condition; it serves to emphasize the state of trial in which we find ourselves as well as the precarious nature of our condition. It is St. Augustine who was right. The "triumphs" of the Church in the Middle Ages were not pure from all alloy, and had a disillusioning aftermath.

So it is that the Church of to-day gives but little thought to a possible revival of her medieval prestige and her domination over the peoples. Her action, as we have seen, has become more discreet, more intimate, less spectacular. She is no less efficient, however, on that account; and indeed such an attitude corresponds better to her present position and to her title of "Church Militant". It is not for the Church a time of glory, but one of humility, of effort, of interior progress. Her rapid growth in the early centuries, her external brilliance in the medieval period were doubtless necessary as a first step towards the penetration of the world by the Christian Spirit. But the hardest, the most mortifying tasks still remain to be fulfilled. Deep down in human society still lurks, almost as strong as ever, the old pagan spirit: its materialism and its cupidity for enjoyment and its cruelty. Our present miseries, in laying bare men's souls, have saved us from any illusions in this matter. The appalling revelations of Hitlerite Germany have placed us on our guard against a naïve optimism about the real state of human progress. In order that Christianity may penetrate the hearts of men it is more than ever needful that the Church should devote herself to her apostolate in a spirit of patience and utter self-sacrifice. For a work of this kind no political hegemony is needful: what is required above all, in all classes and in all milieux, is a living and genuine sanctity.

The Church of to-day has then no idea of preparing on earth, in the near or distant future, for the transformation of her spiritual sovereignty into an absolute and universal supremacy. Entirely devoted to her work of spiritualizing and sanctifying mankind, she unreservedly admits the full sovereignty in its own field, of her temporal partner, the State. It is true that the existence of such a dualism causes her to undergo harsh and tormenting trials. The shocks and complications thus involved may seem to some as sterile as they are exhausting. But this is not really so. The difficulties of the Church's life are a stimulant to her supernatural energies; they enrich her experience and increase her knowledge of men; they are of constant assistance in enabling her to purify the methods of her apostolate. Indeed the co-existence of Church and State on earth provides as it were a providential corrective to the former. The Church, in the course of her history, acts as guardian to the infant nations, she watches over their development, and she reminds adult countries of the Christian principles of justice and of law. But in addition to this she herself learns much from her contact with so many different nations; above all, she sanctifies herself. So, little by little, if we may borrow St. Paul's words, the spots and wrinkles will disappear from her face on earth until the day shall come when, freed from earthly trammels, she will appear all glorious and immaculate in the sight of God.